Making Burros Fly

Cleveland Amory,
Animal Rescue Pioneer

Making Burros Fly

Cleveland Amory,
Animal Rescue Pioneer

Julie Hoffman Marshall

Foreword by Wayne Pacelle,
president and CEO,
the Humane Society of the United States

Johnson Books
Boulder

Published by Johnson Books, a division of Big Earth Publishing, 3005 Center Green Drive, Suite 220, Boulder, Colorado 80301. www.johnsonbooks.com

Cover design by Constance Bollen, cbgraphics
Cover photo: Cleveland Amory Collection, Boston Public Library
Composition by Michel Reynolds

9 8 7 6 5 4 3 2 1

Library of Congress Cataloging-in-Publication Data
Amory, Cleveland
    Making burros fly / Cleveland Amory, Julie Hoffman Marshall.
        p. cm.
    Includes bibliographical references and index
    ISBN 1-55566-346-X
    1. Animal rescue—United States. 2. Animal welfare—United States.
3. Amory, Cleveland. I. Marshall, Julie Hoffman. II. Title.
    HV4764.A58 2006
    179′.3—dc22

                                                    2006010560

*To my daughter, Sarah Madeline,
for taking long naps*

Cleveland Amory hugging a burro at his Black Beauty Ranch (Cleveland Amory Collection, Boston Public Library)

Contents

Foreword

Wayne Pacelle, president and CEO, the
Humane Society of the United States

CLEVELAND AMORY was an animal rescuer on a scale great and small. He and
The Fund for Animals are remembered
for the daring captures and airlifts of
animals that spared them from government shooters and private
hunters. And the millions who have read *The Cat Who Came for
Christmas* remember his effort to bring a stray named Polar Bear out
from the cold and into his caress.

But the heroic kindness of this man went well beyond the rescue of
individual animals in distress. The Fund for Animals, the organization
he formed in 1967 with Marian Probst, advocated and helped to enact
public policies at the state and federal levels. In time, Cleveland became
the instantly recognizable ambassador for these reforms. He hired
teams of lawyers to protect bison, bears, whales, and other animals
through the courts. And he educated millions about the plight of animals, whether through his hilarious and witty television appearances
and lectures or through his unforgettable prose.

His 1974 book, *Man Kind? Our Incredible War on Wildlife,* laid
bare the appalling norms in the hunting and trapping industries and
their handmaidens in state and federal fish and wildlife departments.
His *TV Guide* reviews of ABC's *American Sportsmen*—where he com-
mented on the gravely serious and whispering sportsmen, with backup
shooters deliberately excluded from the camera's gaze, creeping up on
a lounging tiger in India and then shooting the animal dead—shined a
spotlight not just on the cruelty of trophy hunters but on their vain
attempts to make staged slaughter seem noble and even dangerous.
The veil was lifted, and these macho and egotistical men were exposed
as frauds—merciless and pitiful ones, at that.

With his literary flair and Boston Brahmin lineage, Cleveland was well suited to bridge the traditional humane movement, which he discovered and joined in the 1950s, and the emerging and more ideological Animal Rights movement that surged in the 1970s and 1980s. He had a place in his heart for the cats, dogs, and horses and spoke passionately in their defense. And he broadened the national debate over our treatment of animals by challenging hunting and trapping, the use of animals in research, and other institutional forms of animal abuse.

In confronting these abuses, he was unafraid and led the way in a new tactical approach to activism. He vowed "to put cleats on little old ladies in tennis shoes" and to create "an army of the kind" and recognized that sweeping change required a mass social movement.

It's hard for me to be objective about Cleveland Amory. He was a mentor to me, as he was to so many others who shared a passion for animal protection and found a leader in him. When the history of the humane movement in the twentieth century is chronicled, Cleveland will stand with its tallest figures.

Above all, Cleveland was a great man with a common touch. He was not one for complicated philosophical constructs or elaborate theories. His concern for animals was instinctive—a gut-level abhorrence for cruelty. He had no tolerance for a phony or a bully, and he devoted much of his adult life to fighting for the weak against the strong.

He was a man of uncommon gifts who would today be remembered as a great writer and social historian even if he had never taken up the cause of animals. But because he answered that calling, this world is a better place for animals, and those who follow in the cause will always have his inspiration. As Julie Marshall chronicles in this fine biography, Cleveland Amory left a permanent mark on America. And for those of us who were lucky enough to know the man, we'll always smile when we think of him.

Preface

"Man has an infinite capacity to rationalize his own cruelty."
—Cleveland Amory

ONE SPRING DAY in 1980, Cleveland Amory had just pulled his maroon, secondhand Checker taxicab into Central Park South, outside the Plaza Hotel, when he witnessed a carriage driver kicking his horse in the groin. The horse wouldn't budge, afraid of the dizzying city traffic. Violence, apparently, was this man's solution to life's problems, and Amory was happy to oblige him; he grabbed the driver by the throat, preparing to give him a proper New York thrashing.

"You miserable idiot! That animal supports you fourteen hours a day in all kinds of weather. You keep him in a lousy firetrap stable. And when he gets frightened in traffic, all you can do is kick him. I detest you! I'm going to have one of our agents follow you all summer, and if you touch that horse in anything but a loving way, I'm going to see that you get a fine. And if you ever kick that horse in the crotch again, I personally am going to beat you to a pulp."

Cleveland Amory, the father, or more accurately the grandfather, of the modern Animal Rights movement, is an icon and a hero to generations of people who have a compelling concern for their fellow creatures that gallop, roam, swim, slither, and soar above this earth. Some people first knew Amory as the author of three social satire books that rib upper-class Bostonians; others remember him as a commentator and resident curmudgeon for NBC's *Today Show*, chief critic for *TV Guide*, and senior contributing editor for *Parade* magazine. He reached worldwide fame as the author of a trio of cat books based on Polar Bear, the bone-thin, white cat he saved from a filthy alley one snowy

Christmas Eve. *The Cat Who Came for Christmas* (1987) remains the most beloved cat book ever, selling 3 million copies in twenty countries and in various languages, including French, Italian, Portuguese, Swedish, German, and Japanese. With the publication of *The Cat and the Curmudgeon* (1990) and *The Best Cat Ever* (1993) Polar Bear rose to the status of world-famous feline, receiving a great deal of fan mail after gracing the cover of *Parade* magazine and appearing on the TV show, *Entertainment Tonight*. As Amory explained, "Cat books are very personal to people." The author's most powerful words, however, came during his well-publicized and often contentious crusades to save our most vulnerable creatures from the most heinous abuses, under the banner of The Fund for Animals, the pioneering animal welfare organization he founded in 1967.

The first and most far-reaching confrontation Amory led with his Fund for Animals took place in 1979, at a time when the Fund had no money to spare, but Amory trusted his gut instinct and purchased a sea vessel that would sail to Canada, the site of the largest mass slaughter of marine mammals seen to this day. With Amory on board, Captain Paul Watson and his *Sea Shepherd* crew sailed to the Magdalen Islands and went to work in the dark of night, spray-painting live baby harp seals on the ice with harmless red organic dye, thus rendering their soft pelts useless on the market. During the same year, Amory spared 575 burros from sharpshooters in the Grand Canyon in an extraordinarily bold maneuver and one that earned him the title, bestowed by the *Boston Globe*, as the country's "most controversial crusader" against cruelty to animals. Using every ounce of his God-given charm, disarming wit, and widespread influence—not to mention his penchant for annoying the hell out of government bureaucrats—Amory persuaded the National Park Service to allow The Fund for Animals to hire wranglers to rope burros, then airlift the animals by helicopter. If not for his persistence and concern, those live burros would have silently been churned into dog food or fertilizer. Park biologists admit that Amory is responsible for changing the way land managers now deal with wildlife on national park lands—more humanely. After the Grand Canyon rescue, hundreds of sad-looking, floppy-eared animals needed a home, and so came the founding of Amory's legendary Black Beauty Ranch, an animal sanctuary in East Texas teeming with diverse species spared from tragic fates of human cruelty. The ranch is a safe haven to bobcats bought on the black market, chimpanzees used in animal research, and a maimed zoo elephant of such sweet nature that she still—to everyone's amazement—loves and trusts humans. Amory's book *Ranch of Dreams: The Heartwarming Story of America's Most Unusual Animal Sanctuary* (1997) tells many tales of animals saved from horrific abuse.

Amory was an outspoken, fearless, and often outrageous individual, and he brought a much-needed, renewed vibrancy to the Animal Rights movement. Before he came on the scene, the welfare of animals—mostly unwanted stray dogs and cats—had been relegated to elderly women. Animal organizations were ineffective, weak, and pretty much nonexistent in terms of fighting cruelty, which explains one of Amory's most often repeated statements: "I wanted to put cleats on little old ladies in tennis shoes." His followers became vigilant guardians of wildlife and aggressive detractors of hunting—Amory never could understand the mindset of a person who could hug his dog, then turn around and blast a beautiful deer to bits. In the end, Amory did so much more than anyone thought one person could do by spearheading a grassroots organization. Today The Fund for Animals has evolved into the largest animal welfare organization in the nation and throughout the world, given the January 2005 announcement that it has merged many of its programs with the Humane Society of the United States and is now part of a much larger organization with a $96 million budget. Its leaders, however, have vowed that the Fund will remain its own unique, vibrant, and battle-hungry animal protection organization for the future.

All his life, seemingly endless cruelty cases came knocking on Amory's door. Whether it was a prairie dog, a coyote, or a pigeon, no animal was too old, too ugly, or too insignificant in Amory's book. He wanted to bridge that gap between dogs and cats and American bald eagles to show that there is a whole range of animals worth caring about. In fact, the more "lowly" the animal, the more he wanted to help, which was the unique philosophy that set Amory apart from anyone claiming to do humane work—besides the fact that in thirty-one years as the Fund's president, he never took a dime for his work saving animals. Today's Fund for Animals president, Michael Markarian, recalls the time Amory was urging the US government to list the koala bear as an endangered species. Logging and development had wiped out two-thirds of their eucalyptus forests in Australia. "Cleveland said, 'If we can't protect an animal as charming as the koala, what chance do homely animals have?' "

Amory died October 14, 1998, in his sleep of a chest aneurysm in his New York apartment near Central Park. He was eighty-one years old. The last night of his life, the animal crusader worked the phones until 8 P.M. He had always impressed people by picking up his own phone in his New York office, which for many years was the Fund's headquarters, located just down 57th Street from Carnegie Hall. Most appropriate were the words of his longtime assistant and today's Fund for Animals board chair, Marian Probst, regarding his last day on earth: "Cleveland went down fighting."

He parted as a beloved figure worldwide. At the November 12th funeral, held at the Cathedral of St. John the Divine in New York City, the pews were filled and Fund president Markarian gave the eulogy about Amory's global influence: "When Cleveland passed away, I was at an animal welfare conference in Brazil. I announced the sad news to hundreds of animal lovers from Brazil, Argentina, Chile, Colombia, Peru, and other countries, most of whom never met Cleveland Amory, but nevertheless were touched by him in some way. A Brazilian woman told me she started working to protect animals because she read *The Cat Who Came for Christmas* in its Portuguese translation." In fact, days before he died, Amory had sent his very last autographed copy of that book to Markarian in Brazil for a silent auction to raise money for animals.

The multitudes of individual lives Amory touched—humans included—are perhaps his greatest gift. He once said that his ultimate goal was to create an "Army of the Kind," and after more than three decades of fighting in the trenches, his foot soldiers are carrying on his work. It can be difficult, unrewarding work at times, fighting against shameless ignorance and callous indifference to pain and suffering, but Amory trained his soldiers well and groomed them for the day he would be gone. They work in The Fund for Animals offices throughout the country and can be found each day, from sunrise to sunset, caring for the animals at Black Beauty Ranch. The list of recruits is too long to mention here, but includes great generals, such as Wayne Pacelle, president and CEO of the Humane Society of the United States, who has long been recognized as a rising star in the Animal Rights movement. Many of Amory's people went on to form offshoot groups, while others work for different animal organizations around the globe with the knowledge that Amory was the one who showed them that it is possible to fight for a world of greater good for animals and compassion for all species.

Each soldier in Amory's Army of the Kind carries his or her own special memories and stories, and a select few can say they had the honor of standing beside their mentor to face down those who dishonor humanity. Heidi Prescott, for instance, joined Amory against a bloodthirsty mob of people who shot, kicked, and mangled pigeons, all in the name of fun. The nefarious Hegins Pigeon Shoot, held in Pennsylvania every Labor Day, was halted because of Amory's courage and remains one of the Fund's most impressive wins to date. In addition to these memories, there are the sanctuaries; besides Black Beauty Ranch, Amory also left behind a thriving Wildlife Rehabilitation Center near San Diego, California, and a rabbit sanctuary in South Carolina.

If there was one animal trod upon more than any other, Amory would say, it is the rabbit. In fact, when he was musing about his turn at the proverbial pearly gates, he had one question ready for the Supreme Being: "Why didn't you do more for rabbits?"

The big question most often asked of Amory by news reporters and his many admirers was, How did it all begin? His thoughts on this—and many other issues—are safely tucked away, along with all his self-edited manuscripts, photographs, and handwritten letters, in the Special Collections section of the Boston Public Library. Visitors are not even allowed to bring a coat, a notepad, a purse, or a pen into the locked room where one may peruse the Amory files, and there is always an eagle-eyed librarian making sure nothing is torn or otherwise tossed about. Security is a good thing, because within the hundreds of carefully sorted and painstakingly cataloged items stored in large cardboard brown boxes is a rare treasure: a lifetime of work that is a testimony to both humankind's horrific failings and hope for the future.

Most of all, Amory wanted those who cared to share his vision and to realize, as he did, that every instance of cruelty matters, from the terror of the hunt to the misery of the laboratory, for any misguided act that harms another living creature, whether on two legs or four, flippers or a tail, diminishes us all. For the countless individuals who have felt too insignificant to speak out about abuse or felt that their voice would never make a difference, Amory's boundless fighting spirit proved invaluable. He validated the right to question cruelty and do something about it.

Cleveland Amory gives Polar Bear a scratch. (The Fund for Animals)

1

One Bullfight, a Bunny Bop, and a Battle for Life

"Cleveland was more than just a charmer; underneath his humor, he was a serious man, always seeing four steps down the road."
— Marian Probst, Board Chair, The Fund for Animals

BORN SEPTEMBER 2, 1917, in the resort town of Nahant, Massachusetts, Cleveland Amory came into this world destined for greatness. Not the sort of heroic greatness he would later embrace by saving unfortunate creatures from the crosshairs of a semiautomatic, for instance, but the type of greatness one is expected to build upon from birthright. Hailing from a long line of successful Boston textile manufacturers, Amory bore the clear markings of old money—the sort of thing that matters to members of upper-class Boston society, or in his era more appropriately dubbed Boston aristocracy, a term he came to despise. Education from the best schools would be no obstacle for a child born into the Amory clan, and by college graduation he would most assuredly be eating pâté rather than saving the goose that made it.

To best understand his roots, all one need do is take the short and scenic eight-mile drive southwest of Boston to the town of Milton. Since its founding in 1636, Amory's hometown has remained an affluent community, built row upon row of gated homes with finely sculpted lawns and sprawling grand old estates. The town also happens to be the site of New England's first chocolate factory and America's first piano factory. The nation's first railroad ran through Milton and it is also the birthplace of former president George H. W. Bush. Cleveland Amory's name is still well-known here, too, according to

Pat Desmond, publisher of the weekly *Milton Times*. The Amory family included his parents, Robert and Leonore Cobb; his brother Robert, who would grow up to become deputy director of the CIA under President Eisenhower; a sister, Lenore Sawyers; and two other siblings, Priscilla and Frederick, both of whom died in the 1918 influenza epidemic that killed millions of children. While much of the landscape has since been incorporated into the campus of a small liberal arts institution named Curry College, the Amorys' white, two-story Georgian Colonial home still sits atop a knoll at 956 Brush Hill Road, and has been meticulously preserved over the years as the residence of the college's president.[1] Amory spent much of the first eighteen years of his life in this New England retreat, built in 1918 and tastefully designed with a formal library, seven fireplaces, seven bathrooms, a wing for servants, and formal gardens featuring blooming dogwood and magnolias. Amory's favorite childhood memory, he once told a hometown reporter, "was plotting with my older brother, Robert, to get our governess, Miss Quince. We'd communicate by Morse code, thinking of ways to trip her up." The playfulness of the young Amory would be better put to use during his razor-sharp yet boyishly gleeful debates with people who disregard animal suffering.

As a boy, Amory was drawn to animals thanks to a dog-loving aunt and his own DNA. His great-great-uncle was George Thorndike Angell, a prominent Boston attorney who founded the American Humane Educational Society after watching a race that left two famous horses—Empire State and Ivanhoe—dead. In 1868, Angell founded the Massachusetts Society for the Prevention of Cruelty to Animals. He is the namesake of Angell Memorial Animal Hospital, and is also responsible for bringing the first publication of Anna Sewell's *Black Beauty* to the United States. That classic novel wielded a tremendous influence on the young Amory, who would eventually come to build an animal sanctuary in East Texas and name it Black Beauty Ranch after the famed horse who taught people that animals are individual spirits who indeed feel emotions. Amory first learned about the book from his favorite relative, Aunt Lu Crehore from Jamaica Plain, who had a penchant for picking up strays and bringing them home, and he was always angry that people laughed at her for being different and caring so much for animals. "Aunt Lu" influenced her nephew to get a dog of his own, so at eight years old, Amory met his best friend, Brookie.

A young and dapper Cleveland Amory (photo by Bachrach, Cleveland Amory Collection, Boston Public Library)

The Old English sheepdog was the one who opened Amory's eyes to the joyous world of animals; he loved that dog so much, that he figured since his private school was a short walk from home, he ought to take Brookie with him. In his mind, there was no need to ask for adult permission, and in what seemed like a comic skit, the boy shoved his large, affable, long-haired, wet-nosed pal under his tiny wooden desk. Of course the teacher saw it, and Amory sadly took Brookie home. But it was too late, once the dog knew the route to school, for he turned right around and joined the children during outdoor recess. Amory adored Brookie, but after all, he was a boy and most boys his age were shooting birds with slingshots and Sears BB guns. Amory, who at that time was nicknamed "Clippie" by his family, felt horribly guilty after the fact. Never mind that Clippie was shooting at trees when a bird flew over, he once told a reporter. "I aimed, and by rotten luck, hit him." The bird fell to the ground, flopping, and Clippie screamed for his father, who stepped outside, looked at his son with disgust over the sad display on his porch, and said, "You shot him, you kill him." Clippie jumped on the body until the pathetic creature was no longer breathing, and he never got over it.

Amory did not have to travel far for the next stage of his education at the historic college preparatory boarding school, Milton Academy, a three-mile drive from his house on Brush Hill Road. The academy has been home to such distinguished people as US senator Ted Kennedy. Within the school annals reads Amory's academy history under the heading Class of 1935: "Cleveland Amory, age 17. 956 Brush Hill Road, Milton, Mass.: entered school 1929; Day School 1929–35; Orange Club, Music Club 1930–35; Orchestra 1932–33; Hockey Manager 1935; Tennis team 1934, 1935; Orange and Blue Board 1933–35, Editor-in-Chief 1934–45; James Bates Field Prize 1933." Given its charter in 1798 and bearing the motto "Dare to Be True," Milton Academy remains a prestigious K–12 day and boarding school. While the student body has dramatically changed over the years to represent ethnic diversity (13 percent of students are from outside the United States), the physical grounds appear to be the same as when Amory set foot on campus. The original 200-year-old, moss-covered stone wall surrounds a picturesque landscape of rolling green hills and red brick Colonial-style dormitory buildings.

After graduation, Amory went on to join Harvard's class of 1939 and held the prestigious post of editor of the *Harvard Crimson*. He once said, "If you have ever been president [sic] of the *Harvard Crimson*, … there is very little, in afterlife, for you." The Harvard graduate was hired by the *Saturday Evening Post* and at age twenty-two became its youngest editor. A writing career would be put on hold, however temporarily, as Amory was a young man during World War II and he served as a lieutenant in the army's Military Intelligence Division.

Following the war, Amory's first wave of literary fame occurred with the publication of his trio of social histories about what he knew best. First was *The Proper Bostonians* in 1947, a book that remained in print and brought him royalties for the rest of his life. *The Last Resorts* was published in 1952 and eight years later, *Who Killed Society?* In the first book, which was about Boston Brahmin society, Amory offered the country a rare glimpse into the lives of such "old money" names as the Cabots and the Adamses—names that are etched forever on the

The two-story Georgian Colonial home where Amory spent his boyhood still sits atop a knoll at 956 Brush Hill Road in Milton, Massachusetts. (Julie Hoffman Marshall)

ivy-covered walls of New England's most prestigious clubs and institutions. He was motivated to write this hilarious exposé because he got "so damned fed up with all those boring snobs who can only talk about what their grandfathers did." Amory wrote with such rare wit that the *New York Times* opinion editors felt compelled to dedicate an editorial to his satires. Boston high society was so exclusive, for instance, that firefighters who rushed in to put out a fire at the Somerset Club were detoured to the service entrance. Unfortunately, they appeared during the soup course, and had to wait until the main course was finished and it was announced that there would be no dessert because the kitchen was on fire, before they could do their jobs and douse the blaze. By that time two pantries had burned down. It was a world with scant perspective on reality. One story concerned a job reference that a Boston investment firm sent to a Chicago bank for a young man who came from one of Boston's first families: "His father, they wrote, was a Cabot, his mother a Lowell; farther back in his background was a happy blend of Saltonstalls, Appletons, Peabodys ..." The bank replied in a curt letter that read, "We were not contemplating using Mr. [Smith] for breeding purposes."

Amory's *Last Resorts* revealed the private world of exclusive vacation resorts, including Nahant on the north shore, where he had spent magical summers playing Saturday night croquet by Chinese lantern. But he also remembered, not so fondly, the times he had gone swimming at a beach, or rather a point called Forty Steps. He explained during a newspaper interview: "You go down 40 slippery slimy miserable cracked seaweedy wooden steps and you arrive not to a sandy beach, not even a pebbled beach, but to rocks, just plain *rocks* ... And you go into this ice-cold water ... the damndest cold water you ever felt." One morning, a wet and shivering young Clippie stood on a pointy rock and turned to look at his father, a dyspeptic man who had once said, "Nothing good ever came out of a warm climate." Still, Amory took a chance and opened his mouth. "This isn't much fun, is it, Dad?" "It is not supposed to be fun," the elder said, adding that the boy would feel good when he stepped out. Amory adopted his father's surly attitude as well as his cultural background. Call it East Coast style or old world culture; it was a unique, somewhat bleak philosophy on how one should live and was the perfect upbringing for a soon-to-be cantankerous, self-described curmudgeon who would master the use of sarcasm to blast away his critics during animal rights debates. In his third work, *Who Killed Society?* Amory documented the moral decay of society as he saw it. These three books made him a literary star and introduced a wider audience to his stinging wit. Among his memorable early epigrams is "A good family is one that used to be better."

The social history writer was an acute observer of odd human behavior, but it was not until he began working as a beat reporter that Amory witnessed an abominable side of human nature. One hot summer afternoon in 1945, working for the *Arizona Daily Star*, Amory walked across the border at Nogales, Arizona, to cover a story, to witness a cultural tradition, and, little did he know at the time, to spark a personal revolution. Its sister city, Nogales, Mexico, is an attractive town humming with street vendors enticing turistas to haggle for Talavera pottery, carved pine tables, woven baskets, and rugs. But on this day, Amory was interested in a different sort of spectacle. He entered the gate to an outdoor stadium, climbed a set of stairs, and took his seat up high among a crowd of spectators, which included University of Arizona students looking for an afternoon of fun and entertainment based, strangely enough, on an eighteenth-century "sport." The first bull entered the ring and Amory whipped out his reporter's pocket-sized notepad and pen. The journalist's eyes were wide open, eager to see what to him was a mad, unfettered beast, the kind that could split a tree trunk with his horns, charge a freight train, or kill a man on sight. Ernest Hemingway, among other famous authors, had written about such worthy opponents of the matador, spinning legendary tales about the bullrings of early Spain. The bullfight was traditionally depicted as dramatic tragedy, pitting brute strength against the proud, graceful matador on the cusp of his last earthly breath. But of six so-called fights that day, Amory noticed that "not a single bull entered the arena without a care in the world, but to find the nearest way out." The bullfight, it turns out, is less about bravado and entirely about teasing, tormenting, and torturing a bewildered beast, and Amory would later brazenly condemn this so-called sport in his many essays, TV, and radio broadcasts. This was man at his cruelest, in a fight about as fair as the ones the Romans glorified in the Colosseum, but in modern times, "instead of throwing Christians to the lions, Spaniards throw bulls to the Christians."

The festivities began to unravel before Amory's eyes as the first three humans, called picadors, rode into the ring atop blindfolded horses, spears in their hands. From a safe distance the men thrust multiple steel blades into the bull's neck and shoulder muscles, rendering the beast too weak to raise its head. (This was not so safe for the horses, who in typical fashion would soon silently be gored to death. No one would hear their pain, as their vocal chords had been cut out before they set a hoof into the ring.) Then came the banderilleros, or lesser matadors, on foot, who rushed at the bull and stabbed the animal again and again in the neck with barbed wooden darts, enlarging the existing wounds to promote the flow of blood and make sure the job would be done. When the bull had sufficiently slowed its pace and was too exhausted to make any attempt to fight back, the brave, death-defying matador stepped in and attracted the bewildered bull with a dizzying display of flowing red cape. It all ended with the matador striking the final blow or, well, the second blow. No, the third, or the fourth and final blow. Apparently the matador tries and often fails to surgically strike between the cervical vertebrae in order to slice down deep into the heart. *Olé!*

In all fairness the matador did fall down—once. "That time the bull actually carefully avoided him and stepped over him.... But over and over again, each time more exhausted, the bull charged that silly waving cloth—until finally he could charge no more. Then he just stood there, awaiting the final thrust. This, of course, contrary to what you're always hearing about, was no 'clean kill.' Indeed not one 'clean' anything did I see that afternoon." The journalist's summation: Aside from being cruel, bullfighting is about as honest as All Star Wrestling. The matador was no heroic fellow and the bull was no threat. "A cross goose could have killed him." Such a horrific event prompted Amory to do research to uncover what he and hundreds of spectators had not seen that day and what amounted to a series of serious disadvantages to the bull. First, before the fight, the animal is raised by ropes and pulleys so his horns can be filed down, then he is held in a dark cellar until the very moment he will rush into the stadium in the heat of the day, blinded by the sun. Even Hemingway admitted that after the modern picador has done his work, "there is not more bull left to fight." So not only is the bull's fate sealed the moment he is picked for battle, but his dignity is ripped to shreds. If there is such a thing as a defining life moment, this momentous day belonged to Amory. The bullfight literally changed his life; it lit a spark of compassion and became the turning point for a whole new career. He had loved animals as a child, but this event started what he called his real work. Before that would happen, however, the journalist had one score to settle. In the dusty bullring, after the matador had just killed the bull, cut off the animal's ears, and held the bloody, fleshy flaps of skin above his head in a gesture of victory before the crowd, the red-faced Amory leaped from his seat and marched down to the stadium floor. Without a hint of hesitation, the writer dismissed his notepad and pen—and any sign of objectivity—and heaved a heavy, rain-sodden cushion like a bullet at the head of the matador, striking the back of his head. The man in the shiny black, skintight suit toppled over face-forward onto the ground. "I've had a lot of great feelings in my life, but this was the best."

Amory's gradual evolution from author and media celebrity to animal rights activist began in earnest with the bullfight. "I knew then that the end of my career in Arizona was nearing. I never went back to the paper." After that experience, animals forever crept into his numerous columns, television, and radio broadcasts. Amory could have headed in an entirely different direction, using his family name and celebrity connections to become a self-indulgent media star. Actors were hanging on his written word, and he could have exploited that power for huge personal gain and a gratified ego. After all, he had sailed with Princess Grace of Monaco, dined with the jet set at the Russian Tea Room on New York's 57th Street, and on any day his table might have included actors Henry Fonda, Cary Grant, or fellow author, journalist, and best friend Norman Cousins. And his writing talents were in such high demand that the Duchess of Windsor invited him to tea and to ghostwrite her memoirs. His response was honest yet merciless: when the duchess asked for the perfect title to her future book, Amory said it deserved to be called "Untitled." A stony silence followed and that was the end of that. Amory later explained his words, or lack of words: "You cannot make the Duchess of Windsor into Rebecca of Sunnybrook Farm." He had willingly ejected himself from the comforts of social status and family money, and having reached a pinnacle of authorship decided to use his power of the pen to save animals from pain and death. As he liked to say, he went from writing about Mrs. Astor and her pet horse to writing about her horse. Amory plunged headfirst into the deep end of animal rights causes, as the first topic that grabbed his interest was animal research, namely vivisection, or the use of animals for medical, cosmetic, or consumer research and experimentation. "You might say I went a bit afield from where I was born, but you do what's in your heart and there's a big job to be done."

It would be a vast understatement to say it was a difficult time in the 1950s and 1960s to speak for animals being used as research tools. Although the New England Anti-Vivisection Society had, one decade earlier, introduced a bill to prohibit vivisection of dogs and cats in Massachusetts, no one—neither lawmakers nor humane societies—was willing to support it. It was simply too difficult to fight the God of science. The Berlin Wall might as well have been erected between the media and an ignorant public on one side and on the other, a tight fraternity of physicians and researchers unwilling to be challenged on their use of animals. Amory was undeterred, as he wrote about laboratory experiments in his "First of the Month" column for *Saturday Review* and penned several articles for the *Saturday Evening Post* exposing cruelty to animals on a staggering scale. Conservative estimates were that 300 million animals were dying each year in labs. He wasn't just talking about hamsters, rats, and mice—the lowly research subjects that no one seems to care about, although he did—but about millions of dogs, cats, and monkeys being operated on and harmed on a regular basis. What was most impressive to

Amory's readers was not that he ever set out to teach people how to be compassionate, but he educated them about what was going on in the hidden world of animal experimentation, and because of that, led them to do something about it. He did this not by preaching or yelling but by simply citing the many experiments he saw, firsthand, when visiting laboratories. At Harvard University, he saw dogs that were forced to inhale actual flame and were not killed until three to five days later. At Columbia University, researchers struck dogs in the leg with a rawhide mallet to induce shock—as many as 1,000 blows to each canine leg. Those who administered such atrocities wrote up their lab results, stating that three dogs who survived the shock expired the following day when they were again placed upon the "animal board." To Amory the point of all this was greed. Scientists were motivated to use animals in the lab by the draw of easy money—millions of dollars in grants (read: taxpayer dollars) from the National Institutes of Health. Since it was founded in 1948, the NIH has been the largest funder of experiments in biomedical research. In 1955 the government set aside $138 million for grant research and by 1965 increased it to $1.2 billion. In 2005 the amount was $5 billion. Grants help to validate such research as an experiment to determine whether a mother monkey displays affection toward her young. (Yes, she does.) That little experiment cost taxpayers only $1 million. What was even more disturbing to Amory was that because the world of big science is competitive and researchers do not like to share information, all too often cruel acts are repeated, sometimes more than twice. At Creighton University in Omaha, for instance, dogs were deprived of food for sixty-five days before dying. After those dogs were long gone, researchers discovered that the very same experiment had been performed three years earlier—at the same university.

Amory's columns on animal research drew thousands of letters, mostly favorable to making the world better for animals. Florence Morgan of Arizona wrote a letter to the editor at *Saturday Review*: "For a long time I have liked Cleveland Amory's 'First of the Month' column for its fine style, its civilized tone, and its good content. Now he has won my admiration for his courage in taking up the fight against the torture of animals in laboratories. He will probably be assassinated, but he will perish in a good cause." Albert E. Reinthal Jr. of New York wrote: "A million thanks for the column about cruelty to laboratory animals—it was just what was needed. Only a man of

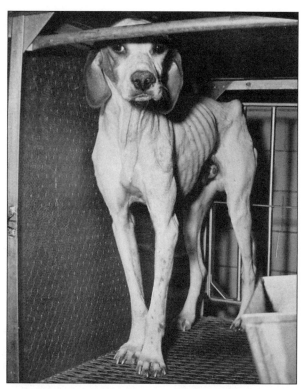

A dog purposely being starved by scientists for research.
Cleveland Amory was one of the first people to document
horrors inside the animal labs. (Cleveland Amory Collection,
Boston Public Library)

Mr. Amory's prestige can blow this thing up to the necessary nation-wide proportions." It appeared that public sentiment was in Amory's camp when a poll taken by the *Philadelphia Bulletin* showed that 40 percent of Americans opposed vivisection. But inside the lab was a climate hostile to speaking out publicly and actually doing something for the animals, as exemplified by signs posted on the wall of one New York lab facility: "Do your best, you can never tell when some antivivisectionist will come around." "Put animals to be discarded in the garbage can." "Watch the incinerator. Live animals have a way of getting into it." Medical ethics and a sense of decency were not required to be part of this institution. What went on in these places was hard to watch. Among Amory's collection of writings and photographs at the Boston Public Library are graphic videotapes. Anyone who watches the one of a small calico kitten, just a few weeks old, with a spark in her eyes, will be horrified. The tape rolls as the kitten, who should be pouncing at balls of string, drags the immobile rear half of her body across a sterile lab table as she hopelessly spins in circles, crying in vain for anyone who will hear her. An 8 x 10, black-and-white photograph shows a a small wire cage containing a large, mixed-breed dog, part black Labrador, that is all skin and bones. His expression reveals he has already given up. Some of the saddest-looking subjects are the beagles, used widely in research because the breed is known to be extremely affectionate, loyal, and loving—apparently you can do just about anything to a beagle and he won't turn and bite you. Amory saw the same dog used for research in Cleveland, Ohio, for nine years, who never once left the cage. A doctor there told Amory that he wasn't sure the dog needed any exercise because each time he walked by the cage, the dog wagged his tail. Amory gave the scientist a strange look. "We need a federal grant to study you."

Amory received many unfavorable letters about his writings, too, from students and researchers in the laboratory. A student at the venerable Massachusetts Institute of Technology wrote: "The very fact that we do kill animals, proves that we have the right." We may be bigger and stronger, Amory would say, but we have no moral right to harm animals. If we find something or someone in outer space that's bigger and stronger and better than us, does it have the right to do experiments on us? Of course not. Amory was labeled a "humaniac" and an anti-vivisectionist, although he never did call for a total ban on medical research that uses animals. He did ask for reform of needless repetitive experiments and for researchers to mitigate pain, use anesthesia, and give animals postoperative care. He wanted them to stop doing research on the same animal again and again. As the world would find out, Amory was not a radical maverick out to destroy scientific endeavors that are for the health of humankind; he simply believed there ought to be a middle ground between antivivisection and research unlimited. Any reasonable person with a heartbeat could know what is over the line. Amory reported on one doctor, for instance, who kept a pregnant monkey in the vise of a restraining chair for two years where she eventually gave birth, remaining rigid the whole time. The scientific purpose of that experiment was to see if it made any difference to the monkey. In a 1964 article, Amory spoke of a visit to a New York hospital in which seventy-five animals who had undergone grim operations were too weak to get to the water left in their pails. The man who was paid to take care of them had left for a weeklong holiday without bothering to put anyone else in charge. Amory always encouraged people to go in and see for themselves what was happening in the lab, to notice the human specimens in charge of the animals' welfare. A glaring example of idiocy he would use during panel debates with scientists was the researchers at Wayne State University who hit dogs with a pneumatically driven hammer to test the efficiency of football helmets. The idea grew from a discussion on whether football helmets are sufficient for football players. One dog, labeled No. 131, was struck fourteen times; taxpayers were charged $131,000. The conclusion? It's best to wear a helmet when you're hit on the head with a hammer. Wayne State was a bastion of animal abuse. Amory found dogs that were operated on and, without postoperative care, dumped in the medical school's basement. Their agonizing howls carried well beyond the university walls all the way to a neighboring hospital where patients there called the Detroit Police Department. A policeman, John Mobley, appeared on the scene and was led by the howls to the basement, where he discovered the grisly scene. Mobley was, in Amory's words, a good strong Irish cop, not a bleeding heart, and yet he was incensed when he saw the abandoned and wounded animals lying helplessly in their steel cribs. The night watchman told the policeman, "No one watches these dogs, and they are only interested in the time it takes them to die." Mobley replied, "If this is called for in the advancement of science, God help us all." The laboratory was closed down temporarily. Amory was outraged by the response of one of the medical school's top administrators and brought it to public light. "Do you know what the dean of Wayne State University Medical College said?" he asked rhetorically during a 1965 debate on NBC. "One, the dogs should not have been put in the basement, the howling dogs; they should have been put in the soundproof rooms upstairs. And two, the dogs should have been debarked [their vocal chords cut]."

The more Amory exposed what was going on, the more it seemed plausible that attitudes were changing. It wasn't just he and his readers anymore who became aghast at what was going on inside the lab. Even vivisectors and physicians were examining their actions and speaking out. After sixteen years of killing more than 1,000 rhesus monkeys for the US Air Force's radiation experiments, Donald Barnes quit his job and joined the national Anti-Vivisection Society. It was ethical blindness, he said, that had kept him from hearing the animals' cries of pain and made him ask himself what he was doing. Another researcher, Dwight Ingle, a physician at the University of Chicago, wrote critically of the "unanesthetized burning of animals" and "the deliberate production of extreme pain," which his community was in the business of procuring. "If experiments of this type must omit anesthesia in order to advance medical knowledge, I am not aware of acceptable rationalization of them. Whatever knowledge is gained by such experimentation is not worth the price." Amory received a poignant letter from a man who asked that his name be withheld from publication, identifying himself as a PhD working at one of the most highly regarded academic institutions in the United States. The writer said he was distraught from witnessing undergraduate students dissecting animals without anesthesia, but with drugs that immobilized them on the table, "for practice" during their spare time. Amory counted on his many letters and his own notes from unannounced laboratory visits for use in numerous debates with vivisectionists. Probably the best example is the infamous "cat, dog, eye" debate televised in Toronto. With just one minute left in the show, Amory shuffled a stack of papers he kept in front of him and pointed to one. "Here's a case where they put the eyes of a dog into a cat. Then they put the cat's eyes into the dog. What possible good could that do?" The pathologist, his opponent, responded: "You don't know the first thing about ophthalmology. That experiment might prevent blindness in children." Amory interrupted, "Don't go on, sir, I made up that example, just to prove that you'd defend anything."

It wasn't only the medical labs that Amory had his watchdog eyes on. In a consumer test at St. Joseph's hospital in St. Paul, Minnesota, researchers funded by the tobacco companies tried to prove that cigarettes are safe by smoking (or not smoking) a dog to death, literally, by the extension of a graft to the bronchial tube through the chest wall. With every breath, the dog was forced to inhale cigarette smoke.

What Amory was asking for, in the form of federal legislation, was something akin to what England had passed in 1876: a law to protect laboratory animals from needless suffering and pain. Stating his case before congressional committees, Amory explained that though his movement was not as powerful as the medical fraternity—the American Medical Association—he was not alone, and he urged politicians to recognize that people who love animals were not yet unified because they tended to be highly individualistic people. Disorganization should not be interpreted as weakness, he argued. He had been in a position to gauge how the public felt about animal rights, and the people demanded a law, because science had wrongly adopted the attitude of "by any means possible."[2] Congress passed the Animal Welfare Act of 1966, the first legislation addressing the treatment of laboratory animals, and to no one's surprise the medical research community fought it tooth and nail. The act was amended four years later to address basic standards of taking care of animals used in experimentation, but it has consistently failed to prohibit painful and cruel experiments on animals.

As a writer investigating and exposing cruelty in the lab, Amory was finding that he could make a difference through his many publications, but not all of his editors were readily accepting the material. He lost his eleven-year position on the *Today Show* after he wrote a controversial piece in 1963 on laboratory animals called "Science Is Needlessly Cruel to Animals." Amory was even more invested in publicizing cruelty in order to stop it, for that year he was made privy to an event of the same magnitude of his first bloody bullfight. The "Sticks-and-Stones Hunt," or the "Bunny Bop," had been occurring every December just before Christmas in the quaint town of Harmony, North Carolina, population 400. Folks would take to the fields in the foothills of the Blue Ridge Mountains, collect sticks that fell from the peaceful willow and sturdy oak trees, and proceed to bludgeon, kick, stomp, and smash any rabbits to be seen to a bloody pulp. All was clearly not harmonious in Harmony.

Amory had heard about the Bunny Bop from a Humane Society worker who had read one of his articles on bullfighting and wrote him a letter, urging him to come to her state and see what this prize-winning contest, sponsored by the local American Legion Hall, was all about. This is what he saw: Men, women, and children surrounded a field and chased rabbits into a central area. When the animals tried to hop away and hide in a bush, they were yanked back and beaten to death with sticks, clubs, stones, feet, or bare hands, and with little or no effort to do it quickly or humanely. Wounded rabbits were tossed to dogs to finish them off, while others, despite fractured skulls and broken bones, slowly tried to drag themselves away. Some bunnies lay motionless yet still breathing. Once, a bunny clubber was trying to smash a wriggling rabbit with the butt of a gun when the weapon

Cleveland Amory snuggles a rabbit, a creature that he felt was most trod upon. One of his first efforts to publicize cruelty stopped the Bunny Bop, an insanely bloody bunny bashing held before Christmas by the folks of small-town Harmony, North Carolina. (The Fund for Animals)

went off and killed the man. Amory stated that the man's death should be listed as "rabbit-induced."

Amory's presence on national television exerted enough pressure to force the legion's president to withdraw sponsorship and call an end to the bloody melee. After the Bunny Bop, Amory lost not only his lucrative job but also friendships with people who could not understand his committment to the cause, and with those who thought he was doing it for fame or had simply lost his mind. He was an animal activist for neither of these reasons, but out of a pure, heartfelt calling, and because he never did anything halfway. His stepdaughter, Gaea Leinhardt,[3] shares the story of one cold New Year's Eve when the family was in the lobby of a movie theater near Times Square, waiting to go in and see *Lawrence of Arabia*, when a cold, wet mess of a puppy caught his eye. In the midst of the crowd, the frightened pup was dashing around the lobby. "It was snowing and really crappy outside, and everyone was acting as if nothing was wrong." Gaea's dad told everybody to go into the movie and the two of them put the dog in the car. The family already had a dog, so they searched for a humane shelter. The frantic puppy and the cold indifference of the theatergoers were disturbing, but so were people's willingness to torture helpless rabbits or to cheer at a traditional bullfight.

All of these events pushed Amory toward a lifetime of animal work, and now he was committed to take the next step. Soon he began joining as many animal organizations as he could. He sat on the board of directors for the Humane Society of the United States and joined the National Catholic Society for Animal Welfare. "I got as high as honorary vice president and that's about as high as a Boston Episcopalian can go," he said. He managed to achieve rank and status as president of the New England Anti-Vivisection Society and continued to bring to light instances of horrific cruelty in medical research. But his independent spirit was telling him that it was time to create a new kind of organization. He envisioned a new force that would be stronger and much more aggressive than anything he had experienced thus far.

Cleveland Amory with a rescued pup, Little White Dog, at Black Beauty Ranch (The Fund for Animals)

2

The Fund for Animals

"I think if you are lucky enough to have something of a 'name'
you ought to use it for something that needs help. Also, if you
are lucky enough to have a voice that has a chance to be heard,
I think it should be used for something that needs that voice.
What needs help more than the actual voiceless?"
— Cleveland Amory

THE MANHATTAN APARTMENT had once belonged to an opera singer, and ever since the new tenants arrived, crescendoing scales had been replaced by the plaintive and no less dramatic meows of the many office cats who came to work each day at The Fund for Animals. There was Benedict, a hefty, sixteen-pound tuxedo who never missed a board meeting unless it coincided with the 4 P.M. dinner hour; Little Girl, a shy coal-black kitten with emerald-green eyes, found clinging to a tree during a storm; and Polar Star, a white cat who extended a paw out of his cage to bat Amory's arm when the latter was visiting a shelter on Martha's Vineyard. The Fund's felines spent their days lounging on stacks of papers (especially those that people were trying to read), leaping onto Amory's lap while he was on the phone, and taking long luxurious naps in any one of the corners where there were cat beds made out of blankets with a pillow on top—Benedict had six of these he decided were just for him.

The apartment was cozy, with minimal space for Amory, his secretary, a bookkeeper, and his longtime editorial assistant. Marian Probst had willingly made the switch from her previous job assisting Amory with copyediting and proofreading TV scripts, reviews, and books to what was now a full-time job as keeper of an animal crusader. She was fond of animals and haunted by a mental image from childhood in Salem, Ohio, where she'd seen duck hunters in the field carrying strings of dead birds flopping upside down. Besides, life with Amory had always been full of unexpected twists. For instance, her boss was nothing like the person she had imagined before their first introduction when *Who Killed Society?* was on the best-seller list. "I featured him as this short man with a mustache in a silk dressing gown. I thought the job would be terribly lah-de-dah and that I wouldn't fit in." On the contrary, Amory stood six-foot-four, weighed 260 pounds, and looked as if he styled his hair with an eggbeater; he wore rumpled clothes and a battered sports jacket, and usually had food stains on his tie. He sat somewhere between unpretentious and downright sloppy, but he could always laugh at himself. He liked to joke that he grew anxious around furriers because they might take a liking to his shock of wiry brown hair that stuck straight out of his head. It was a fitting image for the Fund's hectic and humble beginnings.

The telephone was always ringing at the Fund's headquarters. Someone would call to notify him of an event in Topeka, Kansas, for instance, and ask Amory to come out and give a speech to the women's club. He was always in a hurry to get someplace; once, when he was flying out of Ohio, he failed to notice that he had jumped into the wrong private limousine, where he hollered, "To the airport!" The driver took him, and Amory even tried to hire the man for his next trip. When in a new city, Amory would stay and give a newspaper interview or be the guest on a radio or TV show, partaking in casual banter with the hosts, but the topic always had to be animals. Fans who went to hear him speak would stand in line for hours to shake his hand; he picked up new volunteers and much-needed donations along the way.[1] Amory had started The Fund for Animals with $900 of his own money and was relying on his book royalties to cover his living expenses and pay Probst. He firmly believed that donors had rights, too, and so he was reluctant to spend, asking Probst to log and double-log every cent so no one could come back and say the Fund was playing fast and loose. In fact, Amory had hoped that when he mentioned The Fund for Animals during interviews, people would hear "fund" and send in money, but instead they thought the name suggested there was a pot of money floating around for them. By the time the organization caught the public eye, it was too late to change, and besides, it really seemed to work because it was getting noticed.

In the first two years of the Fund's existence, while he was seated as a guest on the *Tonight Show*, Amory unknowingly reached out to a woman in Michigan whose life would be forever changed and who would help the organization make history. Doris Dixon had fallen asleep with the television on when Amory's distinctive Boston accent brought her out of her slumber. The next day, she called The Fund for Animals. Even though she was a complete stranger, Amory decided he had found his first field agent to investigate cruelty across the Midwest. It was a scenario that would be repeated often, as he had either a great capacity for trust or an uncanny ability to read people and know that they would do a great job, perhaps both. If you loved animals, you were an immediate friend to the Fund and you might soon find yourself in charge of bears in the West or jackrabbits in the South. Your garage might be confiscated as headquarters, but don't expect to be paid, or at least not very much. All Amory seemed to require were profound dedication, a strong mind, and a free spirit. He wanted people who were enthusiastic about making a pioneering journey into animal rights.

Dixon was a private investigator by training, and her first assignment from Amory fit her background well. A friend of Amory's who was running an airline out of southeastern Michigan reported that he had been hired to transport exotic felines from Africa and South America. Dixon, a redhead, went undercover in an outlandish blond wig, toreador pants, and a huge mod belt, playing the part of a middle-aged floozy interested in buying an exotic cat as a house pet. Dixon discovered that it was true: the clients were warehousing animals and sending them to various places for such activities as hunting safaris. She befriended a reporter, Tom Hennessy from the *Detroit Free Press*, and together they published lengthy exposés. Soon thereafter, she was called on to investigate a so-called animal shelter in southeastern Ohio. What she saw was appalling. The owner had set up a drop slot, like that at a bank, for animals that led into a basement. Just two times a week, the owner, who also was the county animal control officer, picked up the animals. It turned out that his wife was selling these discarded animals to laboratories for medical experiments. Dixon gathered evidence, alerted authorities and put a stop to this sleazy business. Her best reward was the beagle-mix she rescued and named Pocahontas. The dog's cry from the bowels of that building had been so pathetic that she had no choice but to crawl down into the dark tunnel and retrieve her. No one had

The burro rescuer hugs one of his favorite animals, and is joined by celebrity Loretta Swit. (Cleveland Amory Collection, Boston Public Library)

stood up to this animal control officer, who was influential, holding jurisdiction not only in Michigan but in areas that extended to Ohio and West Virginia. It was becoming clear to Dixon that the majority of people failed to see the need for animal protection because they accepted the status quo. The Fund had a long road ahead, but she felt positive because her organization finally offered a place for activists with raw passion and untapped energy to make dramatic, meaningful change.[2]

Amory often visited his Midwest agent to give her support, but Amory immediately became a full-time job for her. He was always the first one up at 5 A.M., looking for someone to play chess with; at midnight he might get around to having dinner. It was exhausting and invigorating at the same time, and by the end of the tour she looked forward to the day she could "send him back to Marian." Every trip was invaluable, however, as she learned what it meant to be an effective advocate. Amory and the Fund were being attacked in print all the time, often by outdoor writers—columnists who specialize in outdoor sports and the majority of whom support hunting as a so-called sport. Sometimes the attackers were quick to back down, but one personality, known as Mr. Ecology, was a relentless foe of the Fund. He publicly called upon Dixon to appear on his local Detroit TV show for a feisty debate. It clearly was a setup, so Dixon set him up to debate Amory instead. Mr. Ecology threw out every excuse not to be at the table. When Amory showed up and his opponent did not, Amory requested a hat from the moderator so that he could take on both sides at once. He placed the pith helmet atop his head and proceeded to do his one-man show. First, with the hat, he launched into a diatribe about hunting as a bonding experience whereby the hunter becomes one with his prey. Sure it is, a hatless Amory said, particularly after the hunter is the only one left standing. Dixon, meanwhile, was in the other room, falling off her chair in laughter. Public debate, though not fun for everyone, was second nature to Amory. He played by his own rules and never gave in to a trap. If someone tried to corner him with the typical "animals versus humans" propaganda, he'd respond in kind. If his opponent asked, "If a boy and a dog were drowning, which would you save?" Amory's response was "Well, that would depend, because if the man were Charles Manson, then most certainly the dog."

After several years of Amory shuffling around the Midwest, debating, making speeches and visiting local garden clubs and community centers, his Fund for Animals was about to experience a monumental change that would define its core nature and set its course for the future. It was 1970, and the organization could finally afford its first paid employee, a woman named Patricia Forkan, who was the first person to press the question: "But what are your projects?" The first real project of the Fund was focused on one of the most misunderstood and terrorized animals in the world. The wolf has always been on the

US government's hit list. According to the American Museum of Natural History, an estimated 2 million wolves were killed in the last half of the nineteenth century, by settlers who cleared the way for cattle. By the 1930s most wolves had been shot, poisoned, or trapped. In Amory's time, Alaska had been routinely shooting wolves by helicopter, swooping down and herding them across the flat ice floes where there was nowhere to hide, it was easy to miss, and there was hardly ever a clean kill. In 1971, Amory testified before Congress and helped to pass the federal Airborne Hunting Act—the prohibition of aerial slaughter of wolves and other wildlife—which became law the following year, albeit with some major loopholes. The Fund had found its niche as a voice for wildlife, an area that had never seriously been targeted by groups fighting cruelty against animals.

That same year Amory spoke for wolves, he also testified on landmark legislation that would ban Americans from killing whales, dolphins, seals, and other mammals of the high seas. While he was at the nation's capital, Amory met Lewis Regenstein, who shared his firm belief in the importance of this new bill, called the Marine Mammal Protection Act. Regenstein had political savvy; he had worked for the CIA and also earned a master's degree in political science from Emory University in his hometown of Atlanta, Georgia.[3] Soon Amory asked his new friend to start up the Fund's Washington, D.C., office. The Fund needed some legs for political lobbying, Amory explained, because while it was indeed reaching people through a newsletter and its founder's travels and speeches, it was high time to raise the bar to the next level.

The tiny, one-room office on 15th Street cost $125 a month. It was an old, run-down building shared by many radicals, a quiet woman who sold herbs, and others who could not afford the fancy offices of K Street occupied by lobbyists and lawyers who spent their power lunches at The Palm while Regenstein barely had time to unwrap a peanut butter sandwich. Soon enough, however, as the Fund was raising about $400,000 annually and could finally afford a staff salary of about $500 a month, Regenstein packed up and headed for a two-room office on P Street in Dupont Circle. In one office was the typewriter, which he used to craft his many opinion articles for the *Washington Post* and the *New York Times*, and in the other was a couch piled high with papers, including transcripts of congressional hearings and studies. A short walk down the hall was a bedroom where Regenstein lived. He rarely left because there was too much mail coming in. Even at Christmastime, he hesitated to return to Georgia, fearing that someone would break in and steal the unopened donation checks. Mail was overflowing because of the Fund's direct-mail campaign to support the Marine Mammal Protection Act, which would also ban the import of marine mammal products, including baby harp seal pelts. Regenstein knew the campaign was a highly effective method as soon as he heard that Capitol Hill had received more mail about baby seals than about the Vietnam War. The Fund generated millions of letters. Although now hardly a day goes by without an appeal from a nonprofit in the mailbox, in 1970 direct mailing was a novel concept.

The Fund needed an edge because it faced a tough audience: furriers, government agencies that regulate hunting and fishing, and many supposedly pro-wildlife, pro-conservation organizations opposing the ocean mammal bill. The majority of these organizations was content to support a weak law that would manage the slaughter of marine mammals, but the Fund was one of the few brave voices demanding an end to US whaling operations as well as the destruction of hundreds of thousands of bottlenose dolphins caught in tuna nets. It was a vision that was considered extreme, but in the early 1970s, what seemed to be radical notions of caring about land and water and protecting nature were emerging from US citizens and being framed within landmark legislation. The Fund was a leader, working for the stronger law alongside Christine Stevens, president of the Animal Welfare Institute, whom some call the mother of the Animal Rights movement, as well as the Humane Society of the United States and Defenders of Wildlife. Regenstein had help from hard-hitting editorials in the nation's top newspapers. The Marine Mammal Protection Act, which included language he had suggested, passed in 1972, and is the reason why millions of animals are alive today. One year later, Regenstein helped lead the charge to strengthen the Endangered Species Act, persuading Congress to protect habitat and to broaden the definition of "endangered," to make sure a species receives protection before it approaches the point of being wiped out forever.

Two years and two huge victories made Regenstein believe that nothing could ever surpass the supreme satisfaction he was feeling. The Fund's Washington office quickly became notorious for its tenacity, and the volunteers kept coming, as well as requests from other lobbyists who were too afraid to speak out and wanted the Fund to do so for them. The Fund's press releases brazenly named names and pointed a finger at those who were holding up pro-wildlife legislation, while those lobbyists who secretly appealed to the Fund shouted disclaimers that they had anything to do with it. Regenstein made enemies, too, but to his surprise no one ever sued because the truth, he said, was on their side. Sometimes Amory would come down and testify as needed. "He was like a bull in a china shop." At one hearing, Congressman Don Young of Alaska was so irate at Amory's diatribe that he stormed out. "I sort of cringed, but that was our role, to be on the edge, to tell it like it was," Regenstein said. Amory's antics did make it tough on him to negotiate later on, but they also brought much-needed attention to issues buried from public scrutiny. It helped that Amory also tended to bring celebrities with him, such as actress Mary Tyler Moore, who spoke on behalf of The Fund for Animals against the exploitation of animals. She read the poem, "A Paradox," by Edward Breck (circa 1925), at a congressional hearing on the fur trade:

'Tis strange how women kneel in church and pray to God above,
Confess small sins and chant a praise and sing that He is love;
While coats of softly furred things upon their shoulders lie—
Of timid things, of tortured things, that take so long to die.

'Tis strange to hear the organ peal, 'Have mercy on us, Lord'
The benediction—peace to all—they bow with one accord;
While lights from stained-glassed windows fall on shoulders
    softly warm—
Of timid things, of little things, that died in cold and storm.

The same year that President Nixon signed into law the Marine Mammal Protection Act, The Fund for Animals hired its first West Coast field agent. Virginia Handley had called to ask for more information about this upstart organization that was making waves, and Amory invited her to come out from San Francisco for a visit. He was very interested in something she had mentioned over the phone, something she herself had created, called the Animal Switchboard, a twenty-four-hour hotline with a running list of lost and found pets, resources to find inexpensive spay and neuter clinics, and "everything the lousy pound was not doing." Very soon, Amory would adopt the concept and create the Fund's Animal Switchboard in Chicago. By the time

Cleveland Amory kisses Peg O My Heart, a cat he rescued from a leg-hold trap, and is joined by Jack Hanna, star of the TV show *Jack Hanna's Animal Adventures* and director emeritus of the Columbus Zoo and Aquarium. (The Fund for Animals)

Handley's plane had taken off back to San Francisco, she was already the Fund's local coordinator in that city. Amory later flew out to attend the first Fund for Animals meeting in the West. Sitting among a small group of Handley's volunteers was a woman who casually mentioned she had some garage space. Amory jumped at the offer: "Good, there's our office!"

A postal worker, Handley had the flexibility to spend time building the Fund's West Coast contingent, and very soon, she was headed to the California legislature to face her first battle with lawmakers, who were considering allowing people with disabilities to shoot animals from the back of a truck. Just like her mentor, Handley was determined to go in guns blazing, so to speak, but her ammunition was a list of quotes from Theodore Roosevelt about ethical hunting. In the end, she used a much softer tactic. Amory loved to tell the story of how Handley was seated in the balcony, and with a tiny whisper of a voice made her case that lawmakers should kill the bill. Amazingly they listened. Supporters of the bill and leaders of hunting groups wagged a finger in Handley's face, calling her unpatriotic. But many war veterans came up to her with smiles, letting her know that killing was the last thing on their minds. The win was short-lived, for the state's Department of Fish and Game commissioners flouted lawmakers by allowing the hunting-from-trucks concept within its own written regulations.

Amory's use of field agents was something new and bold for animal rights, and he treated all of his people with respect for their individuality, allowing them to do their absolute best. Nothing ever had to be written in triplicate; each person was free to do whatever he or she felt was right. There was no time to wait around for a board meeting to discuss action because Amory wanted his people to act fast. He showered them with confidence, and they needed it. California, like Michigan, proved to be tough ground to break. The latest news was that the state Department of Fish and Game was allowing hunters to cut the antlers in velvet (before it turns bony) off of live deer. Handley had a fit, knowing it would be painful and bloody for the animals. Somehow she persuaded lawmakers to mandate that Fish and Game consider the humane aspects, not just population numbers, when setting hunting regulations. Under new rules the Fund was also able to halt bow hunting of bears at least for one season based on the trauma to individual animals. Amory rejoiced, "This is a victory for the 98.5

percent of Californians who don't hunt and a victory for the 100 percent of the bears." California quickly became a big target of the Fund, which went on to challenge the hunters' so-called right to trap bobcats and coyotes. The Fund's leader was tired of seeing the small minority of people in California who hunt and trap control the politics of the woods. But he loved coming to the West because he was always up for a bare-knuckled fight. He set up base camp at San Francisco's Fairmont Hotel, greeting reporters and recruiting new members to the Fund. Like clockwork, just before going on television, Handley would say, "Cleveland, your hair," and he'd rake it through with his hands, ready to go.

A continuous theme of Amory's animal welfare career was that he would venture back and forth between direct action in the field and the persuasive power of the pen, and so it was fitting at this time that he would produce a new book. The response was phenomenal: *Man Kind? Our Incredible War on Wildlife* (1974), was an unprecedented attack on the government's war on wildlife and on sport hunting; critics called it his seminal work and readers were stunned, staking claim to an awakened heart, mind, and soul. *Man Kind?* brought to light many of the grim realities about how people torture, torment, and kill wildlife. As a reviewer for the *Christian Science Monitor* wrote: "The reader will not like what he reads; he may shake with pity, anger, yes even with wrath. Yet assuredly, he will read on, so absorbing are the incidents Cleveland Amory describes in a straightforward although often rightly angry vein." Amory wrote of the bow-and-arrow hunt in Oil City, Pennsylvania, in which 300 archers shot five "wild" boar and five Spanish goats released from a truck. He lashed out at people who regularly use animals for their twisted idea of fun, such as the southern "coon on a log" trick, in which men chain a raccoon to a log and throw him in the water to watch him dance, or leave the animal on land to fend off dogs until exhaustion takes over and the raccoon is torn to pieces. The photographs are enough to make one sick, such as one from the West, where a wire fence runs through a vast desert landscape and attached to the wire, as far as the eye can see, are the carcasses of coyotes strung up by their feet. After reading *Man Kind?* no one could ever seriously argue that animals don't need protection from a culture of cruelty. Amory saw a war in need of an army.

The book further triggered a CBS special narrated by Dan Rather, called *The Guns of Autumn*, a ninety-minute window into hunting culture. The highly publicized documentary dissected the hunting lobby and had hunters tell the facts about hunting. In the initial stages of production, Amory called up his first field agent, Doris Dixon, and asked if she might be willing to help the CBS crew do an investigation in the woods of Michigan. She led a producer, assistant producer, and three cameramen to their first stop, Copper Harbor, where bears are habituated to people and feed at a local dump. The bruins are hand-fed marshmallows, only then to be blasted by hunters on the opening day of hunting season. The crew went on to see the slaughter of buffalo in Arizona and waterfowl in Pennsylvania, and captured on film hunters boasting of their high-tech weaponry. When Rather asked one man why he hunted, the latter replied: "It kinda gets in your blood, like an addiction—you know, like drinking or gambling." After the documentary aired, the hunters whined that it was biased against hunting. Dixon's name was trashed in the *National Rifleman*, the magazine of the National Rifle Association, for her role at Copper Harbor. With the help of the Michigan United Conservation Clubs, hunters filed a federal lawsuit against CBS, but they had nothing to whine about because there was no script—this was raw footage of real men who volunteered to be on tape. The judge threw the case out, not willing to set a precedent for censorship of public information.

As a broad-based audience tuned in to hear Dan Rather talk to hunters, and the book that spawned such conversation flew off the shelves, Amory enjoyed a heightened status. He was no longer a lone voice in the wilderness when it came to wildlife. His Fund for Animals was now the nation's number one enemy of hunting, and it garnered publicity, both good and bad. The *New York Times* called *Man Kind?* "a vivid indictment of the hunting and trapping cult. Mr. Amory is one of those rare writers who can illuminate deep moral indignation with hilarious anecdotes and sardonic wit." But in *Field and Stream* magazine, Amory was mockingly depicted as a cartoon angel hovering over the "Kingdom of the Kind." He was dubbed a bunny hugger and a bleeding heart, and his opponents—those who saw hunting as a right and treated it as religion—went so far as to call him a terrorist and then, in hypocritical fashion, make death threats. That was okay for Amory, who believed that someone who doesn't have enemies is "a dull bastard who doesn't have principles."

Like most leaders of great movements, Amory was a complex and controversial character. He admitted that he was a "bad vegetarian," meaning he fell off the wagon more than once, often when traveling and especially with cheeseburgers. Typical of some men of his generation, Amory could be chauvinistic, and on top of that he was a big, hopeless flirt. And when he wasn't happy about something, such as how a field agent's campaign was going, it was time for some scolding. Generally, whenever someone called with a gut-wrenching tale of torturing animals, Amory would grow angry and appear very cold, but it was nothing personal to the humans around him—he was concerned about the animals and what to do, and his mind was at work.

True to his style of not being a fanatic, Amory maintained that not all hunters are "environmental morons," just the egomaniacal ones, men who must feel so insecure in their own skins or inadequate at work that they were compelled to seek out the largest specimen just to hang its head on a wall without realizing they are foolishly plucking the best genes out of the pool. Just the heartless ones who smile at blood sport without regard for the animal's pain and suffering. Just the ones who fathom that flicking the trigger to blast a bear baited with a jelly doughnut stashed in a nearby tree is some great skill. For those hunters who punish animals for their own sick, sad, and sadistic whimsy, Amory had used *Man Kind?* to turn their own logic upside down. With wicked sarcasm he unleashed his take on the righteous killing of hunters themselves. He called it the "Hunt-the-Hunters Hunt Club." Hunters were multiplying, he warned, crowding fields and highways, and it was time to cull them through a conservation plan that was clearly for their own good. Amory called for hunters who shoot with bow and arrow to be shot with bow and arrow, just to see how sporting it really is. Trappers would be trapped and, "if too small, thrown back to live and play another day." No hunter would be shot within city limits, in parked cars, or during dating season. The club had ethical rules, such as "don't drape your hunter on your automobile" and no mounting of heads. Mounting the cap, jacket, or gun, however, would suffice and still be considered good taste.

As an author and activist, Amory liked to step back and let people think about what they were doing with laughter instead of moral outrage, and that endeared him to his fans as well as people in the movement who seemed, to him, to take themselves way too seriously. Sarcasm was his favorite method, because it is a disarming tactic and a great way to make fun of your enemies, especially if they are more powerful than you. He liked to throw an opponent off balance, like an

Cleveland Amory and Art Linkletter share puppy love during one of Amory's appearances on *The Art Linkletter Show* (1963). (Cleveland Amory Collection, Boston Public Library)

unexpected move in his favorite game of chess. He always tried to stay one step ahead, especially in debates with hunters, and always could get the better of them, a perfect example being the time a hunter was stranded on a small ledge. Amory paused midway through a TV interview and with a sly smile said, "I'm rooting for the ledge."

The movement greatly needed a man like Amory, because until he appeared to speak for animals, no one had even come close to possessing the vision and charisma of Henry Bergh, founder of the first humane society in the United States.[4] To understand what Amory meant to animal welfare, then, one must look back at its roots. The concept of caring for animals is nothing new, dating back to 1641, when the Puritans of the Massachusetts Bay Colony published "100 Liberties," or basic rules. "Libertie" 92, for instance, stated that "no man shall excercise any Tirrannie or Crueltie towards any bruite Creature." One can read English lawyer Jeremy Bentham's 1780 *Introduction to the Principles of Morals and Legislation*, in which he argued that there is no legal reason why anyone should be allowed to torment animals. "The question is not," he wrote, "Can they reason? Nor Can they talk? But Can they suffer?" Organized animal welfare groups first sprang up in various towns in the 1860s. In the next century, animal control, rather than preventing cruelty, would be the mainstay of these societies while the use of animals in research, inhumane trapping for fur, and product testing on animals increased.[5] Amory offered something that would dramatically revitalize the postwar animal welfare movement in America. Simply put, no other animal rights worker had ever achieved the same spotlight. His Fund for Animals would be center stage because it was identified with an individual who was a remarkably likable character. Who but Amory would saunter into a room, his own birthday party, trailed by four dogs, three cats, one quail, one rabbit, and a skunk as his guests?

With solid footing in the movement, The Fund for Animals was well on its way, with expanded political reach and a few fiercely dedicated, however thinly spread, field agents willing to cover the East and West Coasts and everything in between. Both Amory and Probst never took a day off, and droves of volunteers came knocking on the door. The Fund had its niche, and even a motto, "Animals Have Rights Too," accompanied by a bill of rights:

> We Declare Henceforth That All Animals Shall Enjoy These Inalienable Rights: The right to freedom from fear, pain and suffering—whether in the name of science or sport, fashion or food, exhibition or service. The right, if they are wild, to roam free, unharried by hunters, trappers or slaughterers. If they are domestic, not to be abandoned in the city streets, by a country road, or in a cruel and inhumane pound. And finally the right, at the end, to a decent

death—not by a club, by a trap, by harpoon, cruel poison or mass extermination chamber.

Amory put all his resources to work for the Fund's next project: reaching women, far and wide, who chose to wear dead animals. While he didn't seem to care about his own fashion sense, he loved to play on societal notions of vanity to get his point across. "When I see a woman in a fur coat, if someone is with me, I say loudly, 'Just what I told you, it makes her look so fat.'" He enlisted big stars, Mary Tyler Moore, Doris Day, Angie Dickinson, and Amanda Blake, to appear in TV commercials with the line "Real people wear fake fur." In a *Reader's Digest* article titled "Must We Use Torture Traps to Get Fur Coats?" Moore spoke out: "Behind every beautiful wild fur, there is an ugly story. The animal is not killed; it is tortured to death. I don't think a fur coat is worth it." The Fund for Animals was the first animal welfare group to alert the public through television and in the pages of national magazines about the inhumane fur industry, as well as animal laboratory abuse, bullfighting, and unethical sport hunting. It was the first to bring celebrities to the cause. It wasn't hard for Amory, whose circle of friends included Jack Lemmon, George C. Scott, and Gregory Peck, to rope in many big names, and the list included Steve Allen, Glenn Ford, Burgess Meredith, and Jimmy Stewart. Megastar Katharine Hepburn became the Fund's international chair, TV personality Bob Barker was its national chair, and actress Gretchen Wyler its vice chair. Barker, the longtime host of *The Price Is Right*, banned fur coats from his prize list, and when he hosted the Miss USA pageant refused to slip the fur coat prize on the winner. The Fund for Animals garnered star appeal, or as one reporter put it, Amory brought "sex appeal" to animal rights.[6] But at its core it was a grassroots organization dedicated to lowly animals much more than to trendy pop culture, and so what happened next made perfect sense. The year was 1978, and a woman named Caroline Gilbert called the Fund in New York to ask for help to save a rabbit in dire need. She did not know how lucky she would be, or that her one phone call would transform The Fund for Animals into a hands-on animal sanctuary.

Amory had a soft spot for rabbits. One of the most exploited creatures ever, hundreds of millions of rabbits are slaughtered in factories worldwide for meat each year, according to the US Department of Agriculture. That figure does not include the hundreds of thousands of rabbits bred and used in drug and cosmetics testing. Our nation remains active in the trade of meat and rabbit furskins with Canada, France, and other countries. The fur-gathering method is particularly grotesque: rabbits are clubbed in the head and decapitated so their pelts may remain pristine. Amory even had a motto in his campaign for the rabbit: "Hope for the hopeless." Gilbert had stumbled upon seven dead and dying rabbits owned by a man who was breeding them as Easter toys. She knew nothing about the species, but had enough sense to know that the oranges, peels and all, that the man left as food were absurd. The rabbits spent each day lying in their own excrement, smelly and dehydrated. She took the animals and was threatened with a lawsuit. At the time, there was no such thing as a rabbit shelter, let alone a rabbit sanctuary, but Gilbert had heard of The Fund for Animals. "Cleveland said, 'You know that man wants you to pay for those rabbits. I know you are going to hate to do that, but just give him some darned money. We have lots of more important things to think about.'" She did what he said, shelling out $2 per rabbit, and on that day signed on to volunteer for The Fund for Animals. Soon the thirty-acre farm she had bought with the intention of raising horses was transformed into a bunny haven. Without meeting her in person, Amory handed over the finances she needed to run the place.

In the beginning the Fund's rabbit sanctuary sheltered and nurtured as many as 200 rabbits. They were laboratory subjects like Victoria, a rabbit who had spent seven years in a cage and, despite atrophied muscles, thrived at the sanctuary. Doc was a crippled baby bunny when a child dropped him to the floor. Six rabbits that looked like skeletons with fur came from a Greensboro basement where they were used to train pit bulls for fighting. Many of the small, timid balls of fluff arrived pregnant and gave birth to tiny dead bunnies. The sanctuary opened its doors to rabbits used to test a cancer drug after the Massachusetts lab went out of business, but most of the residents were victims of human thoughtlessness rather than malicious cruelty. People buy cute, fuzzy baby bunnies as Easter gifts, but few want to keep the adult versions. Not only would people show up at the door ready to say goodbye to their pets, but Gilbert often found strays that were dropped off to fend for themselves. Domestic bunnies are to wild rabbits as pet dogs are to Alaskan wolves: neither can defend themselves in the wild. Amory could never understand the mindset of someone who willfully injures an animal, or drops one off in the woods to fend for itself, or takes one to a shelter for no compelling reason. "Is it too much that when you adopt a pet it needs to be a lifetime commitment? I don't think so! These creatures are dependent on us for security and happiness."

As the sanctuary grew, soon Gilbert was having to turn away injured, abused, and neglected rabbits because she simply did not have any more room. She realized early on that she and her handful of volunteers could not save the world and that she had better pare it down to do a better job for the health of the seventy or so rabbits that were already in her care. As of 2005, the sanctuary was turning away on average a whopping 1,000 rabbits per year. Gilbert chooses not to allow the public to adopt the rabbits in her care because she wants to make sure this is their last stop and a safe home for life. And it is a great life indeed, situated in the shadow of the Smoky Mountains and beneath wild cherry and grand oak trees. Initially the rabbits were kept in cages and had to take turns in the exercise yards, but Gilbert was dissatisfied. She drew a sketch for Amory of a predator-proof enclosure at a cost of $45,000, certain that he would think she was insane to spend so much for a bunch of rabbits. Instead, he told her to get a contractor to build the "rabbitats"—ten-foot-square, wood-framed structures covered in hardware cloth with a red aluminum roof. In the center of each dwelling is a wooden box complete with rear and front entrances because rabbits don't like a dead end. One of her favorite moments was ripping apart the old cages and releasing the rabbits, one by one, into their new, spacious homes. She could have watched them all day long, kicking and running, jumping into the air to twist and dance on a whim. Every winter their homes are covered in a bed of hay for warmth and for doing what rabbits love most: digging tunnels. They dine on fresh salads and vegetables—usually kale or collard greens, broccoli, and cabbage—and every Christmas, are treated to a holiday cocktail of carrots, raisins, apples, and pears. All are spayed or neutered, and each has a buddy—rabbits are gregarious creatures and do better with a friend for life. There is nothing more charming than a rabbit, Gilbert says. They are mysterious, innocent, and pure.

While the sunset swept a soothing peace over South Carolina's bunny haven, Amory felt calm satisfaction that his Fund for Animals was spreading long and winding roots. With his writing career on hold, he was devoting everything he had to the Fund. Gilbert would have loved for him to have a New York rabbit companion, but as fate would dictate, Amory's life was about to be interrupted by a

A quiet moment with his beloved cat, Polar Bear (The Fund for Animals)

chance meeting with a white cat who would endear him to felines forever.

As a self-described dog man and proud owner of two nine-year-old Siberian huskies, Peter the Greatest and Ivan the Terrific, Amory never imagined he'd come to appreciate cats. Here was a man who never failed to travel without photographs of his smiling mutts. Each night, back at the hotel room after another book signing, Amory would lovingly set their upright frames upon his bedside table. But one night in 1978, when he rescued a frightened green-eyed cat, he was transformed. It wasn't a good night, although it was Christmas Eve, cold and with snow on the ground. He was in a curmudgeonly mood, sitting alone in the Fund's headquarters, opening mail, and looking forward to a quiet evening at home with relatives, when he heard a rapping on the door. At the doorstep was an animal rescuer who was desperate to catch a stray living in a nearby alley. She had been trying to catch the skinny homeless cat for days, and tonight was a must-do mission because the super of the building where the cat had been seen had demanded that the doorman get rid of the cat by Christmas Day. Amory and his new friend trudged through the slippery alley, where they saw the dirty, wet cat with a raw facial wound. Amory noticed that the cat was jumping around and playing in the snow. The animal rescuer, with a slice of cheese in her hand, lured the cat as Amory stood behind her, at one point slipping and cutting his own face on the metal bars of a grate. The cat fell for it. Bloody but with cat in hand, Amory headed home.

He volunteered to keep the stray overnight or for a few days until a home could be found. The next day, a woman who was interested in taking the cat home to her daughter came to inspect this potential present, a hissing, unhappy creature hiding under Amory's bed. He promised to clean the cat for her return. After a feline bath and a good toweling-off, Amory did something instinctive—and shocking—he wrapped the cat in his arms for a hug. There was no way this cat was going anywhere. When the woman returned, Amory put on a fantastic show, tossing out a million reasons why she should not want this untamable, horrible kitty. He convinced her. Amory named the cat who had captured his heart and soul Polar Bear. He marveled at this being, who had a strong mind of his own and an enormous capacity for love and affection. Amory loved to tell stories about Polar Bear on his book tours, to remind people to have gratitude and appreciation for the unconditional love that cats can bring. "The most poignant lesson he taught me was to spend quality time with our pets. They wait all day for you to return home. Don't race past them toward a meal, TV, or to change clothes. Give them love and attention. You'll never regret it, for their time with us is way too short."

Amory settled into a new life with Polar Bear in his New York apartment, enjoying Sunday strolls to Central Park for a game of chess. He was about to face his toughest, most heart-wrenching battle at the close of the decade. The year 1979 would momentarily become the Fund's most tumultuous, as its president would make global headlines for sailing north to a world where ice floes turned red each spring from the spilled blood of innocent creatures just days old.

Cleveland Amory feeding burros at Black Beauty Ranch (The Fund for Animals)

3

Painting Baby Harp Seals

*"We wouldn't be out here protecting seals and whales today
if it wasn't for Cleveland's help years ago, which laid the
foundation for our work. He was like a father to me."*
—Captain Paul Watson, Sea Shepherd Conservation Society

THE VAST ICE FIELDS that cover eastern Canada's open seas were sculpted for animals content never to set foot or flipper on land. Here, some of the earth's most remarkable creatures are born and nursed by their mothers on the edge of ice floes that shine like the blue winter sky. It is a magical moonscape of pure white snow and golden sun, softening the sharpest peaks of ice forged by the tumultuous, windblown seas. Those fortunate to bear witness describe it as a solitary universe of profound peace with potential danger at every turn. Ice pans crack and shift to nature's rhythm, opening holes that reveal the dark open waters. And every spring, the tiny, furry creatures appear.

Imagine forty-pound lumps of Jell-O, covered by soft, silvery fur. Some lie still, digesting the fresh, warm, fat-laden mother's milk in their round bellies, while others amble across the ice toward their cousins, seeking comfort in a tight huddle. With the exception of human babies, there is nothing quite as vulnerable as the young harp seal. These furry babes cannot swim or do much more than lie on their beds of ice and, with puppylike barks, call out to their mothers keeping watch nearby. But mother seals offer no protection from the cruelest and most unnatural predator of all. Every spring birthing season, this peaceful Eden turns into a ghastly hell as the two-leggeds arrive in monstrous fishing vessels that crash through the ice, smashing seals in their path. Once their ships are anchored, an army of khaki-clad men with bloodstained orange gloves jump ship to stalk seals just days old. In tightly clenched fists are their chosen instrument of death: a hakapik, a primitive club with spikes attached, like a large and macabre icepick. The two-leggeds casually approach their victims, white balls of fluff, which surprisingly do not flee but often will instinctively wiggle forward in an inquisitive manner toward these tall, dark figures, which to their eyes could be their mothers. Some seals stay put with their backs toward the intruders, intermittently arching their necks to see, round eyes wide open, what is approaching. The curious silence is broken by the sound of a broken skull, much like the cracking of a lobster shell. Without wasting time, the killer whips out a skinning blade and proceeds to slit the animal's throat, slicing downward to strip the seal of his hide. The carcass is discarded as garbage, with purplish red muscles twitching, heart still beating, and entrails spilling out from the ribcage, next to the others strewn across the bloody red ice marking the killers' paths. Mothers return to the spot they left their young to sit and mourn beside the mess that was once a vibrant lifeform about to explore a wondrous new world. The seal hunt is the most chilling spectacle of man's barbarity, and it is not really a hunt because there is nothing sporting about it.

In 1978 the seal slaughter was in full swing, and one man was desperate to do something about it. As a proud Canadian, Paul Watson could not let these men with cold, pitiless hearts define the character of his nation. His passion began innocently, as a child, the day he asked his uncle to take him to the beach to see the seals. There, along the frozen sands of the Northumberland Straits, the child was horrified to discover the lifeless bodies being dragged to the shoreline; right in front of his eyes, a seal killer sauntered over and tore the skin from a still-warm body. The boy locked his gaze on the victim's eyeballs, which were still attached by sinews to a skeletal frame without a hide and reflecting back a deep and dark emptiness. Then he looked into the eyes of the human and saw a similar void where there should have been an inhabiting soul. Another man walked up and sliced the flippers from a seal to prove what a man he was and to make the boy sick. The boy vomited and the killer laughed.

As an adult, the brutality of the seal slaughter still stirred in Watson's soul. He had heard of Cleveland Amory, noticing that he was somebody rare with an unwavering ability to take action and rectify egre-

Captain Paul Watson with Bermuda the cat aboard The Fund for Animals' *Sea Shepherd*, 1979. This ship would sail to eastern Canada to save baby harp seals from slaughter. (Sea Shepherd Conservation Society)

gious acts of cruelty. He knew that at the beginning of the decade, Amory had testified on behalf of the Marine Mammal Protection Act, which banned Americans from participating in the baby seal bludgeoning. So Watson began writing letters to Amory, thirty-three years his senior, asking for help. And he needed help, indeed, because he had been ousted from Greenpeace, the very organization he cofounded in 1971.[1] Watson's passion to save seals had put him at severe odds with Greenpeace bureaucrats, who lacked the backbone to take on the politically charged issue of killing seals on the Canadian east coast. The end result of those days of personal conflict with Greenpeace was that Watson, a sea captain by training, was without a ship to carry out his professed mission to protect the seals. But Watson smiled when Amory had returned his letters and asked to meet him. Amory was not certain what to expect, for Watson had been highly praised by his supporters and vilified by his enemies. The sea captain had shared with him an ingenious plan to sail to the ice fields of the Gulf of St. Lawrence and, while the murderous seal killers slept, to spray-paint lounging seal pups with a red, organic vegetable dye, which would make their fur worthless on the market and would render the "hunt" pointless. Amory expected a man who was half animal nut and half evangelist, but soon found out that Watson was clearly neither. He was a large and formidable man, stout like a heavyweight wrestler and fearless enough to fling his 200-pound frame in front of a baby seal about to be clubbed. But he also was gentle and charming. At twenty-seven years old, Watson was still very much like that wide-eyed kid who had gone to see the playful sea mammals, and he had become even more enamored with creatures who seemed to know more than most humans do about pure and boundless joy.

Watson caught a bus to Los Angeles and, too broke to afford a hotel, spent the night drinking coffee in all-night diners. In the morning he went to the Beverly Hills Hotel to meet his mentor. Amory approached him in the lobby and got right down to business. He was bigger than Watson expected, as well as gruff and to the point. "So what do you need?" Watson suggested a plane so he and his crew could drop to the ice by parachute, but it might be less dangerous to sail. Amory was unfazed. "Okay. Well, go find us a ship and I'll buy it." The Fund for Animals had received a $477,000 donation from an animal-loving widow the previous year, and every last dollar—plus more—would in the end go toward a seaworthy ship. Watson found the *Westella*, a retired fishing vessel docked in London, well-worn and rusted from a lifetime battling the northern seas. He gladly paid $120,000 for the 210-foot, 789-ton ship, which he knew could be cleaned and renovated and take him to the hunt. And so, in the middle of winter 1979, the ship sailed from Hull, England, to Boston Harbor, where eighteen tons of concrete were poured into her bow to enable her to break through the thick ice on the way to the seal nurseries. After a good sandblasting underneath, the true nature of the ship was revealed, as she was made of pure and clean, unpitted metal. Such a good, strong ship was needed because, unlike the sealing ships that follow Canadian Coast Guard ships that break the ice for them, this vessel would be entirely on her own. Watson renamed her *Sea Shepherd*, as she would tend to a flock of innocent ice lambs. Amory, who was present throughout the transformation, and had enjoyed a visit to his hometown, gazed proudly at the *Sea Shepherd*, exclaiming that here was his newly acquired "Fund for Animals Navy."[2]

In February that year, *Sea Shepherd* set sail with thirty-two crew members, including Amory and a dozen reporters, for the Gulf of St.

Lawrence, which is west of Newfoundland and east of the Magdalen Islands. The voyage was a gamble for Amory's team, largely considered a conservative animal welfare group, but Amory trusted Watson and did not care what people thought about it, especially the Canadian government, which by now had caught wind of world media reports of the seal-saving crusade, and was threatening Watson and Amory, warning them to stay away or it would make sure their ship did not reach the seals. When the *Sea Shepherd* stopped to refuel in Halifax, Amory responded by holding a press conference, telling reporters that if those who supported the seal slaughter attempted to block the ship, he had a submarine ready to go. Reporters believed him. In actuality, getting to the site was the hardest part of the plan. It took four days and four nights of pounding at the thick ice, in which the ship would get stuck and then back up to ram forward again. The captain had a hard time knowing which way to navigate and avoid bad ice conditions, because the Canadian Coast Guard would not help. When a Coast Guard cutter did make contact, cruising alongside the *Sea Shepherd*, its crew jeered at them.

Late in the evening of March 9, the *Sea Shepherd* was at a standstill and could not get through. A volunteer crew led by Watson went over the side to begin hacking at the ice with axes just as a severe ice storm blew in. Amory was asleep in the main saloon when, just before midnight, the mate appeared. It was a miracle, the latter reported: the storm had blown through and had broken up the ice. Amory rushed up on deck and, sure enough, there were new passages of water. The *Sea Shepherd* went full speed ahead and just after midnight reached its destination. Amory gazed starboard at the carnage of the day: skinned carcasses of baby seals and their mothers moaning nearby. On the port side however, the animals were still alive, their black noses and downturned whiskers making them look like puppy dogs happily rolling in the moonlight.[3] The crew felt anxious and victorious all at once, having crashed through 150 miles of ice to get to this universe of paradise and hell.

Under the thick black cloak of night, the crew prepared stealthily, beneath the radar of the quiet sealing vessels and their sleeping crews. The Coast Guard ship was silent, too, its officers smugly assuming that Watson's ship was still trapped by the ice miles away from the seal herds. Wrapped head to toe in orange mustang suits that made them resemble a cross between a gas station attendant and an astronaut, and

A *Sea Shepherd* crew member spray-paints a baby harp seal with red dye to render the pelt worthless and spare the animal's life when the seal killers come in the morning. (Sea Shepherd Conservation Society)

with spray canisters strapped to their backs, eight crew members scaled the side of the *Sea Shepherd* holding on to roped ladders. Aided by low-intensity ship spotlights yet hindered by heavy winds that penetrated their insulated suits, the seal brigade tiptoed carefully among the baby seals and their mothers. With hand-pumps they sprayed the first batch of organic dye onto the white, warm canvases. Amory, who was then in his sixties, was not with them for Watson wanted to protect his new best friend and not get him into any physical trouble. Amory did, however, come down to step onto the ice, and pick up a baby seal, and snuggle into its dense, comforting fur for a sense of his accomplishment and, more important, for a media opportunity. Within twenty-four hours, that Associated Press photograph was sent worldwide to show that The Fund for Animals had made it onto the ice. Back aboard the ship, Amory could see the crew, mere specks in the distance busily spraying through the night until daybreak, by which time more than 1,000 pups sported bright red dye on their backs. The color, along with their white coats, would be shed in a week. Success was short-lived, however. The quiet was violently shaken by the whirr of helicopters—six of them—belonging to officers of the Canadian fisheries ministry, the Quebec provincial police, and the Royal Canadian Mounted Police, who were joined at sea by the Coast Guard cutter's now-awake crew. Helicopters chased the members of the seal ice patrol until there was nowhere to go without falling off an ice pan into the cold sea. The crew was rounded up and arrested, one by one, and brought aboard the enemy ships. The painting expedition was over. Amory stood over the bow of the *Sea Shepherd* and stared out at the crushed skulls, brain matter, and guts of skinned seal pups. He bellowed within earshot of an *L.A. Times Herald* reporter that as God was his witness, he would see this tragedy come to an end in his lifetime. Watson made a prediction as well: this was the first ship to enter Canadian waters on behalf of baby harp seals, and it would not be the last.

Government officials maintained that the seal hunt was being carried out humanely. The means by which seals could be killed were clearly defined, at least on paper. Amory saw a different story of the Magdalen Island butchers. "I've run into one hell of a bunch of cruel bastards in my day, slob hunters, elephant-killers, bullfighters, bunny-bashers, horse-whippers, all of them thugs and cowards, every one, but that bunch in the Magdalen Islands—they take the prize for the most savage, brutal, and unforgivable acts of cruelty on God's green Earth!" Live seals hooked to a tall gaff (a sharpened steel hook on a pole), sometimes through the eye, were dragged across the ice. They were shot, stockpiled, and left to die. Others were clubbed, then hooked through their jaws, and finally reeled in like fish. Seals were kicked and tossed and live fetuses were ripped from the womb. No rules or regulations, in fact, required that a sealer must kill the animal quickly or painlessly, so there was plenty of writhing on the ice. Overwhelmingly the sealers' method of choice was the barbaric hand tool rather than a bullet, because each hole subtracted $2 per pelt, which would then be processed into the lining of sports jackets, gloves, and boots, mainly exported throughout Europe. Perhaps it was the rationalization of killing as a business that desensitized the clubbers to the great pain they caused. Beyond profit-driven motive, however, the seal killers—Canadians and Newfoundlanders, none of them indigenous peoples hunting for food—rabidly defended their work as a time-honored tradition. Amory had heard such rationalization of killing before by the matador in the bullring, but defined it instead as machismo, or men refusing to show empathy with animals out of fear they will be labeled weak and effeminate. The ability to openly show concern for animals, Amory believed, is one of the most *human* things a human being can do. Still, some people, he observed, such as the bunny bashers in Harmony, were not only deadened to the pain and suffering of animals but actually enjoyed it as a mob-style, bloodlust phenomenon. Historically speaking, the Judeo-Christian principle of humankind's dominion over animals has always presented a monumental obstacle for animal activists. The definition of *dominion* is up for grabs, however, and Amory chose a stewardship approach, lauding responsibility as part and parcel of having dominion. His sense of responsibility was not only to be kind to individual sentient creatures but to protect the species as a whole. By the time of Amory's sailing adventure, the harp seal was in serious trouble, and even the government's own scientists were calling for a ten-year moratorium on killing in order to recover population numbers. When Europeans first landed on the east coast of Canada, there were an estimated 30 million seals in the northwest Atlantic—migratory mammals that range between Canada and Greenland—and now more than two-thirds of that population had been wiped out by overhunting.

By the afternoon of the first Fund for Animals seal-saving expedition, Watson and seven of his crew had been taken by helicopter to the Magdalen Islands jail. Amory flew in by helicopter to aid their rescue by appealing to the Canadian government to relocate the arraignment to a less hostile place, but the men would be judged on the islands, charged with interfering with the hunt under the Seal Protection Act, as well as with resisting arrest. Canada's ever-changing rules were infuriating, and what the police chose or chose not to enforce was clearly deemed to benefit the sealers. For instance, officers strictly enforced the rule that no one, without a permit, could dock a ship or land a plane within a halfmile of the seal herds. Of course, animal welfare advocates who applied for permits were swiftly turned down. The media, too, were prohibited from filming or photographing the hunt. Watson and Amory knew it was foolish to depend on this government to solve the problem. While they awaited trial, Amory returned to the island hotel and sat in the bar with the locals as well as with international journalists who had been aboard the *Sea Shepherd*. He was extremely fortunate to get a flight out that night because an angry mob of islanders and sealers attacked the journalists and screamed that they

Cleveland Amory holding a harp seal pup, 1979 (The Fund for Animals)

were looking specifically for Amory. The mob searched throughout the night and were not happy to hear that he had paid Watson's $16,000 bail. The captain was free after five days. Back in New York, Marian Probst made dozens of calls to find a charter company that would carry the rest of the crew out of enemy territory. It was a costly expedition on all fronts. Amory quipped to reporters that it would have been cheaper to just spray-paint the officers.

Amory wanted the world to see what he had seen and brought the seal campaign beyond Canada's borders. He aired footage on both *The Dick Cavett Show* and *The Art Linkletter Show*. He also directed the Fund to get involved, asking Regenstein, its executive vice president, to be in charge of sending out direct mailings from his Washington, D.C., office. Regenstein made it his personal mission to drive Canada crazy, telling caring Americans to send letters directly to the prime minister. Any donations were immediately funneled back into the seal-hunt protest. It was a good time to be an activist, as young people were flocking to street-level political action to change the world, and Amory caught the leading edge of that surge with a broad and varied campaign to expose the exploitation of living sea mammals. Billboards, posters, magazine advertisements, and film footage of gorgeous white-coat seals just four days old with their mothers suckling them, juxtaposed with after shots of the adult seals lying beside the mangled remains of their pups, obviously grieving, had a dramatic emotional impact. The public was enraged and came to care even more when celebrities, such as Brigitte Bardot, took to the ice. The seal hunters however, were organizing to combat the growing sentiment across Europe and the United States that baby seal hunting is wrong. The Newfoundland and Canadian governments funded a traveling theater group to spread their pro–seal hunt message through stage performances. But what bureaucrats did not expect was for their road show to be followed by Amory and another legendary animal rights leader named Brian Davies; the two worked in tandem to hand out film footage and photographs of the hunt, and held press conferences along the way. Davies, a Brit who had emigrated to Canada, founded the International Fund for Animal Welfare in Montreal. If Amory was Mr. Animal Welfare in America, then Davies was his counterpart to the north, despite their different styles. Davies is a soft-spoken gentleman who rather enjoyed Amory's brash and confrontational demeanor. Together, these men were instrumental in creating a wave of consciousness about the seal massacre in their respective nations and around the world. They lived by the motto that organizations don't make change; people do. Organizations are just the vehicle to take you there, but members of groups, and especially their leaders, ultimately have to do the hard work. International pressure at last forced the European Economic Community in 1983 to ban the import of white-coat pelts from one-week-old seals, before they begin to molt and turn spotty silver and black. In 1988 the Canadian government announced that it had banned the baby harp seal hunt altogether.

    The end of the seal slaughter would prove temporary, as the killing would resume in the mid-1990s, and at a more bloodthirsty pace, reinvigorated by better seafaring technology and pernicious predation by Canada and its supporting countries. New markets for seal skins and body parts would be part of the equation, but what would truly frustrate conservationists, marine biologists, and animal welfare advocates was the Canadian government's claim that harp as well as hooded seals, who eat codfish, must be killed in order to recover the Atlantic codfish industry. (See Chapter 8 for more details on the seal campaign, a major effort of the Fund.)

The seal campaign thrust The Fund for Animals upon the international stage and pushed Amory into the spotlight for his crucial role in what remains the world's largest protest against animal cruelty—and the biggest win in the history of the animal welfare movement. As Amory had predicted, the seal campaign was not the last time he would interfere with the hunt, nor was it the end of the *Sea Shepherd*'s adventures at sea. The ship that Amory's Fund had purchased would sail on that summer to a new and highly dangerous mission: to search for and sink the pirate whaling ship the *Sierra*. This ship and its crew were loathed by conservationists and accused by ecologists of disregarding international whale-hunting laws by randomly butchering a

The rogue whaling ship *Sierra* has seen its last days at sea after being rammed by *Sea Shepherd*. (Captain Paul Watson)

Baby harp seal pup just days old on the ice and a prime target of sealers (Brian Skerry, the Humane Society of the United States)

protected species. For at least a decade, the men had routinely harpooned whales—about 25,000 of them—including nursing whales and their infants, then sliced off the whale meat and tossed whatever was left overboard. Watson had to persuade Amory to finance and then support his plan of action, and he did a stellar job on both accounts. The rogue whaling ship was just off the coast of Portugal when Watson alerted his crew of sixteen, both men and women, of his intentions to ram the ship, which was a quarter mile from shore. The captain sailed to land, dropped off all but two volunteers willing to take part, and sailed back out to meet his enemy, a 683-ton vessel heavily loaded with explosive harpoons. The *Sea Shepherd* remained unarmed.

When the determined sea captain told Amory of his plan to destroy the whaling ship, the latter told him two things. He was not to go about it in such a way that the two ships wound up entwined together, allowing the whale killers to jump onto the *Sea Shepherd*'s deck and harm or perhaps kill someone. And seconds before the strike, he was to put a mattress in front of his body because the jarring impact might loosen the superstructure of the sea vessel and send him tumbling over onto the deck. "Paul, of course, always does what I tell him to do," Amory joked with a reporter. "No, make that sometimes does what I tell him to do. No, make that once in a while." In any case the two ships never got stuck, and he did grab a mattress and bring it on deck. But when Watson saw that one of his volunteers was without adequate padding, he donated his mattress.

With its bow packed with sixty-three tons of cement and gravel, the *Sea Shepherd* was on course for an astonishing display of seamanship. First came the earth-shattering blow to the *Sierra*'s bow in an effort to shear off the harpoons, then Watson steered a 360-degree turn to ram his target just forward enough to tear a six-foot gash in the hull. A mad rush of seawater flooded into a compartment loaded with whale meat. The *Sierra* limped into port sporting two gaping holes, its captain an impotent spirit, as he vowed the ship was out of commission as a whaler forever. Not a soul on board the *Sierra* or the *Sea Shepherd* was injured, and the hole in Watson's bow was a relatively small one. Amory was quick to announce that while The Fund for Animals did not condone the random ramming of ships in the open ocean, in this particular case there were two important factors to keep in mind: First, the illegality did not begin with the *Sea Shepherd*, it began with the *Sierra*, and second, whatever one feels about the action, one can still admire the courage and skill it took for three volunteers to take on and defeat the *Sierra*, with its forty-two men armed with knives, rifles, and machine guns. It is a prime example of the Army of the Kind and its soldiers who try to be kind, decent, and fair at every turn, but when the enemy is none of those things, they will fight back in a creative manner.

Watson was arrested and a judge ordered that Amory's ship be given to the Sierra Trading Company. Watson could not tolerate a ruling that he lose his ship, and later scuttled the *Sea Shepherd* by sneaking on board at night and opening the air valves. With help from The Fund for Animals, he purchased a new vessel and continued to seek new animal-saving adventures for his own organization, the Sea Shepherd Conservation Society.[4]

While the *Sierra* was slowly sinking into the abyss, another battle in the world war on wildlife was brewing, and Amory was about to enter center stage. Far from the tumultuous waters of whale-killing captains and seal murderers, in a land of scorching dry heat below massive canyon walls, a four-legged creature was being targeted for destruction. Amory was about to travel to the wild American West, where the working principle for managing wildlife had long been: If it's not working, "shoot, shovel, and shut up." In this case it was not wild cowboys but government biologists, who had decided that they'd had enough of a particular animal thought to be defiling the habitat in a national park. The Fund for Animals would continue to help the Sea Shepherd Conservation Society with finances and advice whenever solicited, but it was time to move on to the next crusade and the burros of the Grand Canyon.

4

Grand Canyon Burros

*"Only when we learn to live and let live with our fellow
creatures will we finally learn to live and let live with each other."*
—Cleveland Amory

THE SEA CAPTAIN was a natural ally from the beginning as caretaker
of the seals, and so it seems strange that the next man Amory would
embrace as a trusted partner had spent his formative years roping
cows, branding calves, and shooting at mountain lions—a lifestyle
that was inherently at odds with Amory's philosophy of speaking on
behalf of animals. Dave Ericsson is a true cowboy in every sense of the
word, belonging to the last of a generation of men who grew up
breathing the dust, sweat, and blood of the western cattle ranch. He
looks like someone who has spent his life in the saddle. It is a beautiful thing to watch him at work, guiding his best horse across the steep,
rocky switchbacks that surround his Arizona ranch, pushing a bull
that has strayed from the herd toward home. With a flick of the reins
held in his worn and callused hands, and a swift kick, the cowboy
sends his horse into an explosive, downhill gallop with sharp turns
along the way to stay in line with the wayward bull. Rider and horse
seem relaxed, moving in a synchronized rhythm with every hoof beating the ground. It is as if they are one creature, like the mythical cen-
taur, but with a lasso rather than a bow and arrow.

Without his horse Ericsson walks a slow and steady, uneven gait,
the result of three knee replacements and a broken back from wilder
days of rodeo bull riding. He'd never complain but just pour himself a
tall glass of whiskey to take the edge off at the end of the day. He

never fussed, for instance, when the doctor told him he could not ride for at least a year after a terrible accident in which a green horse he was training reared up, fell backwards, and crushed him, prompting a flight-for-life helicopter ride. Two weeks after returning home from the hospital, Ericsson was back on his horse, proving his mental toughness was matched by a healthy dose of stubbornness. In that same vein, Ericsson has strong opinions about the way the world is and ought to be. He hates the "goddamned environmentalists" and the young, khaki-clad government land rangers, whom he refers to as "short pants" and who poke their noses in his business if it involves grazing on leased public lands. But despite the occasional annoyance, Ericsson would never give up this way of life, because he's doing what he loves. At the end of the day, he'll head into the ranch house, untie the dusty scarf around his neck, pour himself a drink, and settle into a well-worn lounge chair with a yellow, dog-eared book by cowboy writer Elmer Kelton, a man who "writes like cowboys talk," Ericsson says, and who has a deep respect for the land. So the evening years ago when the telephone rang and on the other end was the voice of a Yankee animal-lover, this western cow puncher was definitely taken by surprise. The government, the voice said, wanted to gun down burros in the Grand Canyon, and not just a few, but all the ones who roamed the depths of the canyonlands. Amory had asked everyone in the rodeo world and then some, and all pointed to Ericsson, a champion roper, as the only man on earth who could pull off such a rescue.

The same year as the Canadians were sailing toward the seal slaughter, the National Park Service was talking about aerial gunning of burros. Amory was enraged. Just as with Alaskan wolves, shooting stampeding burros from the sky is not a precise art, as gunners often hit the spine, the legs, or the tail. Ericsson had witnessed this sort of government-sanctioned burro hunt before. "I've seen one with 15 bullets in him, just trying to die." It's an age-old method among federal wildlife managers attempting to "control" or "harvest" wildlife, namely coyotes in the West, and The Fund for Animals had always vehemently opposed it. The overall plan for the Grand Canyon burros was not management but extermination, pure and simple. Nor was it good science, since the National Park Service was peddling one environmental assessment report as its rationale that the sorrowful-looking, long-nosed, long-eared animals had to go because they were not from this area, or as the biologists like to say, they are "exotic."

Historians claim that the burro probably came from Nubia, an ancient country between Egypt and Ethiopia. More than a century ago, gold miners first brought the burros, also called donkeys, into the canyon as pack animals, and when they were no longer needed, the animals were set loose and multiplied. Park biologists were bitter about burros that thrived by stealing plant life meant for bighorn sheep and other native wildlife. Jim Walters, a Park Service resource manager in charge of the Grand Canyon burros, was instructed by park superintendent Merle Stitt to get rid of them. Walters announced that his agency was looking for a quick, expeditious route to a "direct reduction mandate," so the plan was, in his words, to just shoot and open the carcasses up, and let them recycle into the environment.

Such disregard for life, plus the fact that no one thought the burros were anything special, made Amory want to save them even more. The Park Service called them a "nuisance." Well, Amory thought the Park Service was the nuisance and pointed out the annoyingly schizophrenic relationship the Park Service had with the Grand Canyon burros: there was a time when the agency seemed to embrace the critters—at least where profit and public image were made—by filling its gift shop shelves with Marguerite Henry's 1951 children's book, *Brighty of the Grand Canyon*, about a fictional lonely little burro of the Grand Canyon and his adventures. According to the cover, Brighty befriended "a grizzled old miner, a big-game hunter and even Teddy Roosevelt. ... But, when a ruthless claim jumper murdered the prospector, loyal Brighty risked everything to bring the killer to justice." The book was a favorite among tourists, and a statue of Brighty dominated the entrance to the canyon's visitors' center. Once the Park Service decided to shoot the burros, however, Brighty was long gone from the gift shop and the statue was plucked from its precipice. Its present mission to eliminate the burro was not an isolated event, as the agency was, at the time, engaged in a long and bitter war against these animals of the Grand Canyon. By the time Amory got involved, federal rangers had destroyed nearly 3,000 burros since 1924, the last shooting occurring in 1969, a time Walters describes in a taped interview in the park's archives: "we brought in military helicopters and we shot every burro that we could find. And we thought we got them. ... For a period of about a week the Rangers would go out on board a military helicopter, as I said, and [they] shot an incredible amount of burros, several thousand, and again they thought they had gotten them all out of the Park."

Cowboys thundering across rocky terrain deep in the Grand Canyon to rope a burro. The crew was hired by Cleveland Amory to capture and airlift the burros out of the canyon and prevent the Park Service from executing a fatal alternative. (Dave Ericsson)

Burros were not completely without protection. Congress passed the US Wild and Free-Roaming Horses and Burros Act in 1971, labeling horses and burros "living symbols of the historic and pioneer spirit of the West" and noting that they "enrich the lives of the American people, and that all free-roaming horses and burros shall be protected from capture, branding, harassment, or death." But the law fails to reach burros on public lands that are a perceived threat to ecosystems and therefore would not shield the Grand Canyon burros. In 1976 the Park Service first announced its hunt-and-destroy policy, the media reported it, and the public responded by sending in 14,000 letters of protest. Walters personally received thousands of these, plus a lot of hate mail from people who don't like to see animals killed. After threat of a lawsuit by the American Horse Protection Association, the Humane Society of the United States, and the Committee to Save the Grand Canyon Burros, the secretary of the Interior called a temporary halt and sent the Park Service back to the drawing board.

For the next four years the agency offered up further environmental studies and public hearings. It asked the public to consider a variety of options, including burro sterilization and euthanasia with drugs via a dart gun. According to one report, should a shooting program be needed, park rangers would be flown by helicopter to the general vicinity of the burros. Rangers would approach on foot to within less than 100 yards and "dispatch" the animals with rifles. Mechanical silencers would be used in areas of the Tonto Plateau directly below high-visitor-use places on the rim. Public feedback was sharply divided: some environmental groups and pro-hunting agencies supported the killing while horse and burro advocates, animal welfare groups, and a contingent of park visitors opposed what they saw as unwarranted cruelty. The Arizona Wildlife Federation wrote a letter to park superintendent Stitt, supporting the plan for its scientific objectivity. A hunter from Winnetoon, Nebraska, was ready to pick up a rifle and jump in. He wrote: "Although I suspect you have all the personnel necessary, I feel so strongly about this that I would be willing, even anxious, to volunteer my time and energy in any way. I am now planning a backpacking trip to the Grand Canyon for October." On the save-the-burros side was the International Society for the Protection of Mustangs and Burros, which considered the mass slaughter of the burros an alarmist tactic by a government seeking an easy out from managing them. The Wild Burro Protection Association questioned the science that indicated burros threaten other wildlife, citing information from behavioral ecologist Patricia Moehlman, who believes burros do not threaten bighorn sheep. The Humane Society of the United States raised skepticism over the labeling of burros as exotics, given that they have evolved over more than 100 years to essentially fit in with native species. The agency further questioned the idea of sneaking up on such large, skittish creatures and carrying out a humane, one-shot kill.

In the end the Park Service decided to stick with its original plan. In spring 1979, the agency was to allow a group of sharpshooters and their high-powered, silencer-equipped rifles to eliminate the burros. Amory and his fledgling Fund for Animals asked everyone to step back, take a breath, and allow his organization to attempt a tremendously risky operation that most everyone, including Bruce Babbitt, the state governor, thought absurd. The Sierra Club, the National Wildlife Society, and the National Audubon Society, too, expected the plan to fail, as these wildlife protection groups supported the shooting management plan. Amory wanted to airlift the burros, one by one, from the depths of the Grand Canyon, which is nearly one mile deep from rim to river. It would be a daunting task, given that the canyon covers 1.2 million acres (1.5 times the size of Rhode Island) and the three main burro herds roamed more than one-tenth of the area. Once again, celebrity status played a role, and backing Amory this time were such heavyweights as Princess Grace of Monaco, Angie Dickinson, Steve Allen, Glenn Ford, Burgess Meredith, and Mary Tyler Moore. The Park Service relented and decided to at least give Amory a trial run: he and the Fund for Animals had sixty days to round up thirty burros, before federal rangers went in with guns. The government had decided against staging its own roundup because of the cost, estimated at $360,000 to capture versus $30,000 to kill. Besides, rangers had tried once before to herd burros out of the canyon, but the opportunistic critters always managed to bolt before nearing the rim. Tranquilizers had failed, too, as darted burros scurried up sandstone cliffs and when the drugs took effect, fell to their death.

As the first order of business, Amory sent his southwest coordinator, Richard Negus, to visit the site and survey the plan's financial feasibility. After looking the problem over, Negus, a Brit, asked Amory if he would be willing to spend $280,000 or so "to rescue donkeys from a bloody great hole in the ground." Amory took a helicopter tour of the canyon and said yes, he would. It was no easy statement, for the Fund was still trying to make up for all the money spent on the seal crusade (the Fund was so poor that Probst and the staff were sleeping on the office floor), but Amory was so enraged about the burros that he could not stop. In the end it was geography, more than any mean-spirited criticism or shortage of funds, that proved to be the real obstacle. The Grand Canyon is a majestic rift carved by the raging white waters of the Colorado River and sculpted by Mother Nature in the form of rockslides, mudslides, wind, and snow over millions of years. It runs 277 miles from Utah's southern border to Nevada, ranging from scorching desert to cool piñon pine and juniper forest. Mesas and limestone-crowned buttes stretch toward the sky as if speaking to the gods of an ancient world. Anyone standing on the rim at dawn or dusk is treated to a wondrous feast for the eyes as the sun dances across massive redwall cliffs, glistening in hues of pink and red, orange and blue. But for a man on horseback chasing wild burros the

Burros rest in a corral at the rim of the Grand Canyon, while a chopper gently lowers another burro in a net sling to the ground. (Cleveland Amory Collection, Boston Public Library)

canyon is simply unforgiving territory. Any cowboy will tell you: a wild burro makes a horse look slow and clumsy thundering across a desert maze of spindly trees, thorny brush, and mammoth-size boulders; burros are sure-footed, and, despite their reputation, not at all dumb. Ericsson knew this, because before receiving the call from Amory, he had roped 2,000 head of wild burros for the Bureau of Land Management. "Them son-of-a-guns will duck right, then left; they are smart, very smart. Just ask those hundreds of people who have tried to catch them and have caught none." Amory had to try. His success would set an important precedent because then, there would be no cause to kill burros roaming less treacherous terrain. If park rangers decided to hunt burros on foot rather than showering bullets from the sky, that would not necessarily be humane, either. At thirty-nine years old, Ericsson was willing to take the job and help change the fate of the Grand Canyon burros. He had never tried to rope any wildlife in the canyon, but if someone was going to do it, it might as well be him.

On a hot August day, around 3 A.M., the roundup began. Ericsson started the crew early, because by 10 A.M. the canyon floor would rise to a scorching 120 degrees. "It gets real hot in those red walls; you bake in there." Five wranglers from Wickieup, Arizona, dressed in leather chaps and broad-brimmed black hats, joined the trail boss in a camp on the South Rim. They worked in shifts, in the early morning and in the evening by moonlight. The cowboys brought in twenty-four horses wearing rubber spats to protect their fetlocks from the barbed thorns and rocks. A helicopter pilot with the skills for navigating the canyon's severe winds and thermal updrafts was needed, so Ericsson approached a Vietnam veteran who called himself Chopper Dan. The pilot was not too sure at first, thinking that the guy in the big black hat was insane, but he eventually agreed and the two men became friends.

Ericsson and his cowboys went to work in Cottonwood Canyon, one of many small canyons of the Tonto Plateau. One cowboy would drive his horse in, making an explosive charge at a band of burros, while another would ride up, swing his lasso overhead, and with a flick of the wrist slip the loop around a burro's head. A third rider would then come around the burro's flank and slip his rope around the hind legs. The key was to ambush the burros before they heard anyone coming, because if they smelled or heard someone, they'd be gone. More often than not, a few stragglers would head for high country and perch on a rock overlook. During these precarious moments Ericsson sent in his hounds—six dogs of a Native American breed called Catahoulas who in Ericsson's mind were the real heroes of the Grand Canyon burro rescue. In some respects Ericsson trusted his dogs more than he did people. Two of them, Jake and Blue, were the stars of the canine crew, but all were trained to deftly traverse rocky slopes and herd the wild animals to safer ground.[1] While it had been risky for Amory to hire a man who competed in rodeos, an activity that he felt terrified and exploited animals, Ericsson clearly showed signs of respecting and, more importantly, not abusing his working animals. He also proved, as a team roper, that he could do the job without cruelty. Though roping livestock in the rodeo is an aggressive, unpredictable competition that usually ends in a cowboy-versus-cow wrestling match on the ground, team roping is one of the more graceful events in the corral. In team roping, one cowboy swiftly ropes the head; another catches the rear legs. Both lassos are pulled taut, forcing the cow's body to fall, ever so slowly, onto its side. In the Grand Canyon, team ropers instead walked their burros to a makeshift corral to await the helicopter. Each burro was in turn gently laid in a net sling, soon to be dangling from the chopper by a fifty-foot cable. It was the first time wildlife had ever been airlifted, according to faculty of the airlifting program at the University of California at Davis veterinary school, which sent its students to help Amory by offering medical care for the captive burros. In the first week, thirty-four burros were airlifted to the rim, where the students rushed to meet them and conduct routine health checks.

The rescue ran smoothly, but made for plenty of tense moments. There was the nagging question of what to do with bands of burros deep in the gorge, closer to Las Vegas and Lake Mead than to a cleared area for liftoff. The burros would have to head down the Colorado River, so Ericsson's crew built a plywood corral with steel panels atop a pontoon boat. A boatload of burros riding the rapids was quite a sight. Every day brought a new kind of challenge, as one step in the wrong direction could prove fatal. One horse, a very good one by Ericsson's standards, stepped off a cliff and the cowboy riding her jumped out of the saddle just in time to see his horse fall off the ledge backward. Although only one horse died, the burro rescue was rough on all the horses, and it was even harder on the cowboys having to

Dave Ericsson on horseback and Cleveland Amory watch over burros that will soon be sent downriver to a safer spot for airlifting. (Dave Ericsson)

find ways to chase down wily critters who roamed from the mouth of the canyon to deep in the gorge, from piney plateaus to desert brush and river country. It is tough enough just to hike the Grand Canyon—tourists descending the dirt trails into the mouth of the canyon are greeted by large posted signs that read something like: WARNING: DO NOT ATTEMPT TO GO TO THE BOTTOM OF THE CANYON IN ONE DAY OR RISK EXHAUSTION, DEHYDRATION, AND DEATH. Going down is the fun part, but day hikers seem to forget that the return hike is a steep, thigh-burning climb that never seems to end.

The escapade was a life-changing event for Dan O'Connell, alias Chopper Dan. A thirty-five-year-old city boy from New Jersey, he was operating a sightseeing tourism business in the canyon when Ericsson called. He was up for the challenge: one day he actually roped a burro from the helicopter. It all began as a joke, really, but it worked. First he cruised up alongside the burro, flying about forty miles per hour. His passenger, a cowhand, threw out a short rope tied to a 100-pound anvil, the kind used to shoe horses. The anvil flew out the door and became an anchor, dragging the burro's hooves to a halt. The cowhand jumped out and threw a net over the animal, and Chopper Dan airlifted him back to camp. Sometimes he would pilot the bellJet Ranger—essentially a police department helicopter similar to those that broadcast traffic news from the sky—a scant four feet from the ground, steering among the cacti, and then would turn it and sway, nearly tossing passengers out the door if not for their harnesses. It wasn't for the fainthearted.

Government officials were still a nuisance, spying on the camps while hiding behind mesas by day and peering over cliff tops by night. One night, Chopper Dan and the crew heard a thump, as one of them fell off a cliff. The burro rescuers were not too alarmed, as it was a low cliff, and they concluded that the guy had gotten up to go to the bathroom and lost his way.

In the end, 575 burros were successfully removed, costing a total of $500,000. Donations from the Fund's 200,000 members helped to save them. While Amory's critics scoffed at spending that much money on relatively few animals, his adoring fans were multiplying, having heard about the event through the media, including more than one large spread in the *New York Times*. He was changing people's hearts and minds when it came to the value of an animal's life. After the final four animals were airlifted out of the canyon in 1982, Arizona's Governor Bruce Babbitt, one of the early skeptics, hiked in to show the state's appreciation for what Amory had done.[2] Amory felt very pleased with his historic win, considering the long and lugubrious history of the brave little burro. It was the kind of story no one could imagine ever happening again—not even Ericsson, who grew to admire Amory, first for having the guts to go on television and tell people what he was planning to do (Ericsson said it was a real good thing that Amory had no idea just how easy it would be to fail) and second for being genuine (Ericsson was impressed that every day, even when there were no TV cameras, Amory was there sticking it out till 4 A.M.).

The next big question was what to do with hundreds of wild burros. Some went to celebrities, such as actresses Angie Dickinson and Cindy Williams and banjo picker Roy Clark. Most simply went to caring individuals such as Vicki Claman, a New Yorker who had just retired with her husband, Allyn, on forty acres in rural Connecticut. The couple, both fifty-two years old, were bored and looking for something to do when Allyn saw an article about the rescue. Vicki exclaimed, "Donkeys, that's it!" and dialed the Fund's headquarters right away. Amory visited the Clamans as well as dozens of others around the country who wanted burros as pets, to make sure that none were looking to start a meatpacking plant. He set adoptions at $400 to weed out unscrupulous folks who might sell the animals as pet food, and some of the money went to the Clamans and other caretakers to help pay for hay and veterinary care. Nobody would get to touch a Fund burro who did not have the animal's welfare at heart.

The first truck brought 28 burros of all sizes and colors, including brown, gray, red, and white, to Connecticut. Altogether the couple took in 400 animals and invited the public to adopt. They received hundreds of calls from interested people, and screening became a necessity: some folks wanted a burro to mow the lawn; others planned to warehouse the animal in their garage. Every burro found a home, with the exception of three individuals the Clamans wanted to keep as their own. Solo, a flea-bitten burro who came to their farm a bedraggled mess of skin and bones had to be hand-fed antibiotics through a turkey baster. He grew into a gorgeous, 800-pound gray, black, and white burro who still spends his days in the pasture beside his brother, Prince. These truly are pets for life, since a domesticated burro can live forty years or more. It was important that every potential caretaker see the burro as Amory did: a charming creature with a soft, wooly coat and big, soulful eyes. Vicki was an easy sell after a tiny burro she named Baby came over and sat on her lap the day after he was born. Amory turned a photograph from that day into the Fund Christmas card the following year. Vicki grew to admire all the animals she watched on her farm, noticing their instinctual drive to form tight friendships and stay in inseparable groups. The Grand Canyon burro rescue changed not only the way many people would forever view burros, but also the way wildlife would be managed thereafter. Grand Canyon National Park wildlife biologist R. V. Ward recently noted that because of Amory and his Fund for Animals, land managers are now forced to recognize the power of public opinion—as it should be, since these are public lands.[3]

Today's visitors to the Grand Canyon can peer off Mather Point and explore Cottonwood Canyon and the Tonto Plateau, and ask themselves how in the world the team did it.[4] Then they can head to the gift shop to look for Brighty, who reappeared after the rescue.

Ericsson has his own reminders, including a collection of dusty, black leather-bound photograph albums that tell the story, including a moment captured in 1979 when he and Amory sat side by side on a grassy patch on the South Rim. The opposite page bears a handwritten note from Amory, who sent the cowboy a timeless, "superb hug." The albums sit on a shelf next to his signed, yet unread, hardcover copy of *Man Kind?* Inside, Amory wrote in blue ink: "For Dave who roped a rabbit but let it go! Proving, on his fortieth birthday, he can't be all bad!" Every once in a while, though, Ericsson reaches for a faded album at the end of a long day while his dogs howl in the dark, starry night, and thinks of his unlikely friend. "He was a good man, I miss him."

A band of burros and lifejacket-clad cowboys riding the rapids of the Colorado River. (Dave Ericsson)

Sunny, a rescued collie, pauses at the entrance to Black Beauty Ranch. (Julie Hoffman Marshall)

5

Black Beauty Ranch

*"Put yourself in the animal's place—and I don't mean just the
companion animal—but the horse on the farm and in the wild.
Then maybe there will be more compassion in the world."*
—Cleveland Amory

Although the Clamans and other compassionate volunteers temporarily sheltered burros emerging from the Grand Canyon, The
Fund for Animals had hundreds more in need of a home—fast. Well
before the last burro was airlifted, Amory began searching for the
ideal sanctuary with a forgiving climate, flowing rivers, and abundant grazing lands for his wooly refugees. In January 1980 the Fund
purchased eighty-three acres in northeastern Texas, a property that
included a 1930s farmhouse with a nonworking bathroom. It was
rustic, but that is what Amory wanted: unspoiled land where animals could be free to live as naturally as possible. One of the first to
arrive at the ranch was a female named Friendly, the burro Amory
loved most. He met Friendly in the corral atop the canyon where she
nuzzled her long nose into his belly. Friendly is still at the ranch,
pushing thirty, and is with hundreds of her kind from the Grand
Canyon and even larger rescues in Death Valley National Monu-
ment and at a naval weapons training center in California's Mojave
Desert. This time around, though, federal land managers have been
working in tandem with the animal activists, willingly sending up to
100 burros each year—more than 1,000 individuals in all that
would otherwise be killed—to Texas where they are currently up for
adoption.[1]

Black Beauty Ranch—since renamed the Cleveland Amory Black Beauty Ranch—is exactly as Amory had envisioned: burros wander wherever the mood takes them, often up the driveway of the ranch manager's house to enjoy the shade of the carport. The more social ones try to board the school tour buses, setting a hoof or two partway in the door. Visitors are welcome on Saturdays, but generally this is a closed sanctuary—no animal shows here. Over the years the Fund has been able, through donations, to purchase adjoining fields, and the ranch now encompasses 1,620 acres, with a guesthouse and an astonishing array of animals, such as deer who will lick a visitor's nose, without the foggiest notion that hunting season has begun—on the other side of the fence. A lemur named Punkin lives for a loving scratch under his soft, brown chin. All of the animals here endured injury and pain before finding themselves in this most unusual and peaceful place. The ranch is located a good two hour's drive east of Dallas, past the multilane loops of mega-highways, where roads become narrow and gray concrete turns to green rolling hills. Small towns come and go along the way, but just past Murchison along a county road is a small green and white metal sign shaped like a burro, attached to a fence, indicating that it's just a few more minutes to the ranch's towering, black wrought-iron gate and its double-winged entry adorned with the final words of the classic novel: "I have nothing to fear; and here my story ends. My troubles are all over, and I am at home." Inside is a world of creatures no one would ever expect to see thriving in the middle of cattle country. The list is a virtual Noah's Ark: 2 alligators, 1 bearded dragon, 133 deer, 1 eland, 2 ferrets, 110 guinea fowl, 217 horses, 5 iguanas, 5 llamas, 15 macaques, 1 nilgai, 10 ostriches, 38 Peking ducks, 25 ring-tailed lemurs, 2 siamangs, 1 tapir, 3 wolf hybrids, 1 zebra … and that's not even close to half of the resident species. As Amory liked to say, "It would be a horrible world if everything were on two legs."

Beyond the meandering burros and miniature ponies is a distant field of knee-deep grass, where an unusual gathering of animals seem to find comfort in one another. Ariel, an oryx shunned from the herd at a zoo, is never far from the belly of Cisco the giraffe. Joining them is a group of camels, including Omar, a baby rejected by his mother, bottle-fed, and sold as part of a Christmas nativity scene. Omar didn't even know he was a camel, having never met one before coming here, but one late spring he came nose to nose with his kin and immediately fell in love.

Deer, emu, and ostrich prefer one another's company at the ranch. (Julie Hoffman Marshall)

Rounding out the motley crew is one lucky antelope who was thrown off a trophy hunting ranch for missing a horn and is understandably skittish around humans. Opposite the field, where the driveway narrows into a walking path, are several large fenced enclosures and the home of Sergei, a mountain lion, who stretches his paws inside his bed, a cool construction sewer pipe. Sergei limps across the grass to the perimeter of his fenced enclosure not stiff from a nap but from a botched declaw surgery at the zoo. His roommate, Katya, a female mountain lion, walks a bit strangely as well, after surgery for a blood clot that left her back paralyzed. After three weeks of physical therapy and spoon-fed baby food at the ranch, the puma was still a bit wobbly and so, four times a day, one of Amory's most respected staff members here, Alfredo Govea, walked beside her, supporting her tawny belly with a sheet and holding her tail for balance, until one night her back leg muscles trembled, her tail twitched, and Govea knew it was time to get out of her enclosure as swiftly as possible. With wide amber eyes

Cleveland Amory and his pal, Friendly, who is nearly thirty years old and still lives at Black Beauty Ranch. (The Fund for Animals)

Katya glares at her neighbor, Robert, in a curious yet slightly annoyed manner, and it's no wonder because the baboon is just plain nuts. Robert spends much of his time running in circles, while his roomate, Willy, a pigtailed macaque, searches for any opportunity to grab hold of a pants leg or a limb from any passerby. It's this sort of craziness that can afflict animals who grow up in the research lab. Nearby, Kenya, a ring-tailed lemur who adores a sprig of cilantro, takes a wild leap off a platform to snuggle beside the fence for affection from a Fund volunteer. The one-year-old was sadly and illegally kept as a pet by an ignorant human who stashed her in a tiny birdcage. At the end of the path is a wood-framed pole barn, home to an animal with a personality to match her size: Babe, a 3,400-pound great African gray elephant, stands still while Govea rubs her large round ears and broad shoulders. She makes a gurgling sound, almost like a cat's purr, while her soft, curly eyelashes blink. This elephant is at ease, but her disfigured leg is a sure sign of an earlier, troubled life. Born in a South African national park, she was carried off to the circus after a poacher shot her nearby mother. While chained in an undersized crate, the young elephant broke her right ankle, which now curls backward, resembling a clubfoot. Babe is never chained at the ranch and comes when called, especially if it's time for her daily bath with a low-pressure fire hose. She will lift a leg, without Govea asking, to get a good cleaning.

No matter the size, shape, or manner, every animal is special at Black Beauty Ranch, a place that may smell, sound, and look like the plains of East Africa, but this is rural East Texas, and so it is fitting that the animals that far outnumber anyone here are the horses. Although they may seem quite plain compared with the eye-catching pumas, their numbers and variety are impressive: thoroughbreds, Arabians, Peruvian pasos, Morgan crosses, and wild mustangs.

On a cool November morning around 6:30, ranch manager D.J. Schubert loads his pickup with bags of horse feed and heads out to pasture. It's another peaceful start of the day, driving through a thick canopy of oak, pine, and sweet gum trees that line the long and winding dirt road. Shadow, Schubert's newly rescued red Chow mix whom he found wandering on an isolated stretch of road in a nearby town, sticks his head out the window and nose in the air, smelling the fresh green growth covering the open fields of wheat, rye, and oat grasses that glisten in the morning mist. The truck rolls past Boys Town, a piece of land allotted to 250 male burros before they were neutered last year. Breeding is a big no-no at the sanctuary, which has enough mouths to feed. Operating costs range from $700,000 to $1 million each year. (Imagine 40 loaves of bread a day for just one elephant.) Veterinary care alone costs a pretty penny, and fortunately a local veterinarian in the nearby town of Tyler has zoo experience. On a typical day the animal doctor treated a lemur hematoma, performed dental surgery on a horse, and cured an eland with a bacterial infection.

Schubert takes a sharp left turn into an open field. The rumbling motor attracts a colorful parade of red, brown, black, and butterscotch horses with ears perked and tails swishing in the wind, signs that these animals know it is time for breakfast. It is mind-blowing to realize that none of these horses, many of whom have been used and abused as tools for hunting, racing, managing livestock, or pleasure carriage rides, reside on this ranch to serve humans in any capacity. No cowboy tells them when to gallop; none bears saddle marks anymore. It is a special opportunity to sit back and observe, see how horses form cliques, and be able to determine which stallion will take over the herd, just as he would in the wild. Burros are accepted within equine circles, but horses seem to speak their own silent language. As Schubert reaches for the feed bags, Sabrina, a lean and old, dark brown jumping horse with an injury who is known to be very bossy, sticks her flaring nostrils into the back of the truck to take a big whiff. She peels back her lips, gnashes her teeth, and bucks at any of the other horses who get near the feed, or dare to lower their heads into the metal trough before she has had her fill. Some ranch horses require a bit more than food. Every sunrise for the past several years, Schubert can be found outdoors helping a large sorrel with severe arthritis get up and onto her feet. Another mare, a former racehorse, needs special help after going blind. Her previous owner had pocketed the insurance money that was supposed to treat her eye infection. Then there is Black Beauty, a stunning, solid black horse with a birth defect that makes her cross her front legs as she walks. Add to this list six horses who were six months old and quite sick when the Fund rescued them from a farm that produces Premarin.[2] And then there are the nearly 100 wild mustangs who came to Black Beauty Ranch, saved from the federal government's controversial roundup program. The Fund for Animals is in the midst of a high-priority campaign and an exhausting battle over the treatment of wild horses, and Black Beauty Ranch remains a vital part of its success strategy.

Horses and burros in the lush, open fields at Black Beauty Ranch in East Texas. (Julie Hoffman Marshall)

The national tragedy began a century ago, when more than 2 million wild horses and burros roamed the open range, but cattle and sheep ranchers who viewed horses as competition—some would say vermin—in grazing pastures were unbelievably cruel. They poisoned water holes and wounded stallions, either by shooting the lead animals' eyes out or sewing their nostrils shut, so that when released, the horses wouldn't have the oxygen needed to thunder across the plains and lead their herds to safety. Sometimes men on horseback would simply drive a herd over a cliff. Most of the last remaining wild mustangs—a number hovering somewhere around 25,000—can be found in Nevada's desolate desert and mountains, but also in Wyoming and California, with smaller groups spread across the western states. Mustangs tend to be small, standing five feet tall at the shoulder. They come in all colors— bay, sorrel, roan, black, paint, white, and black with shades of copper—and they are often scruffy, or as one government wrangler put it, tend to be "all haired up." The agency in charge of wild horses today, the Bureau of Land Management, is not in line with protecting living symbols of the free spirit of the West, but rather

Babe, who became an orphan after her mother was shot by a poacher, gets a mouthful of fruit from Dawna Epperson at Black Beauty Ranch. (Julie Hoffman Marshall)

engaged in managing the herds toward extinction, as it continues to round up several thousand animals each year to get them off the land permanently.[3] The Fund believes the bureau is endangering the very survival of wild mustangs, as its roundups pay no regard to gender, social order, or the genetic viability of severely thinned herds, pared down to thirty animals in some cases. The process itself, as Amory put it, is reckless and ill-considered. Helicopter pilots haze a band of wild horses from the sky toward wranglers who herd them into a corral. These roundups break up families and take away dominant stallions who watch over the mares and foals, sire and defend offspring, and lead herds to water. One can imagine the stress on pregnant mares and all the horses who are so high-strung to begin with that they can barely be touched. The bureau does not have to do this, as it has the power to create wild horse areas on public lands, but it will not do so, nor has it ever issued an environmental impact statement to justify a program in favor of livestock grazing and removal of horses. What seems to be at issue here is a powerful, influential sheep and cattle lobby that has a stranglehold on lawmakers and the bureau, because while the bureau manages more than 175 million acres, horses graze on about 5 percent and sheep and cattle graze on about 90 percent of pastureland. In other words, not much has changed from a century ago.

Even more abysmal is what happens to the horses once they have been trapped. The agency adopts out about 8,000 horses and burros a year through its Adopt-a-Horse program—or what Amory called "a cruel stab in the back to American wild horses." Auctions are held throughout the country where for $125, anyone can take home a yearling, filly, colt, or older horse. After a year of probation, the adopter is granted title of ownership and is supposed to care for that horse for life, but the bureau has openly admitted in court that it has released thousands of horses to those who slaughter them, sometimes within weeks or even days of receiving title. Selling a horse to slaughter has become a sure way to make a buck: about $1,000 for a decent-size horse. In 2004 more than 90,000 horses, including thousands of wild mustangs, were killed and packaged in one of three federally sanctioned and foreign-owned slaughterhouses in Texas and Illinois. The demand for horse meat comes from Europe, where there is a growing market in light of mad cow and hoof-and-mouth diseases that have devastated livestock, and where one can walk into a French or Belgian butcher shop or bistro and order up some *cheval*. It is eaten

Little Elvis, one of three bobcats at Black Beauty Ranch, has a big personality. (Dawna Epperson)

in parts of Asia as well. The US Department of Agriculture predicts that we will soon see an increased demand in the export market, too.

The bureau refuses to accept responsibility for what happens to wild horses, comparing horse adoption to purchasing a car: once you have title, it's nobody's business. It has even made it easy to slaughter horses by waiving fees, bending the rules, and operating under a don't-ask, don't-tell policy. For instance, it granted one horse farm 460 horses, despite a rule allowing only one horse per person, and the horses were then shipped to a livestock sales yard. Soon thereafter, 49 of those horses were confirmed butchered in Canada. Another year, the horse adoption program, which costs taxpayers $16 million annually, could not account for the status of 32,000 adopted horses. With its longtime ally, the private law firm of Meyer and Glitzenstein in Washington, D.C., the Fund was able to help persuade a US district court judge to require that adopters sign an affidavit, under penalty of perjury punishable by $25,000, with up to five years in prison, stating that they have no intent to sell a wild horse for slaughter.[4] Even with this new rule, not a whole lot has changed, because the bureau never has made much of an effort to ensure that adopters sign the affidavit; in some cases the document is not even part of the adoption packet. Meanwhile, the bureau has continued to round up more horses than it can adopt, with more than 21,000 horses being held in temporary facilities. Hundreds of horses go to slaughter every year, and on average, one titled adopted horse is sold to slaughter every day, without a single prosecution. (No one has figures on the additional horses that are sent across US borders to be slaughtered in Mexico and Canada.) The adopters claim they never realized their horse was going to be killed, but those in the business say you have to be a moron not to know where your horse is headed. Even more incredible, the bureau allows those who turn a horse into meat to be eligible for another adoption. The latest bad news is a law crafted by Montana's Republican US senator Conrad Burns, passed in 2004, that explicitly allows the sale and immediate slaughter of wild horses if they are ten years old or have previously been on the auction block. This law has opened the floodgates for wild horses to be sold and resold in days. In April 2005 a minister from Oklahoma bought six wild horses fresh from roundup, supposedly for a church's troubled youth program, and brazenly sent them to Cavel International, a Belgium-based meatpacking plant in

A capybura is the largest rodent in the world, and several live at Black Beauty Ranch. (Julie Hoffman Marshall)

DeKalb, Illinois. Here, as in the other equine slaughterhouses, horses are shot in the forehead with a gunlike captive bolt; it's the same method used for cattle.

While the Fund is fighting in Washington and in the courts to keep wild horses in the wild and off the dinner table, Black Beauty Ranch offers a permanent reprieve to some of the herds that were headed for death. In winter 2003 the ranch saved dozens of wild horses the government had planned to ship to a livestock auction. Given only a few days' deadline, the Fund raced to rent large transport trucks and drive to Crescent Valley, Nevada, to pick up the fifty-seven stallions and two mares—the ones who appeared the most ragged and unadoptable—and bring them back to the ranch, where one mare gave birth to a healthy colt who gallops alongside her mother.[5] In this case the government simply let the Fund have these wild horses, which was fortunate, because with rare exceptions the Fund does not buy animals, it rescues them. No one wants money to be a driving influence in the important work of animal rescue. To pay for food and health care, the ranch has devised creative gift-giving ideas: anyone can donate money to feed a wild mustang for a week, two weeks, or up to a month in the name of a gift recipient, who receives a certificate honoring him or her for caring about safe haven for our last wild horses.

If awe-inspiring, free-roaming horses represent the heart of Amory's Black Beauty Ranch, then it is the smart and ever-amusing chimpanzees who are its soul. Every morning, Fund staffer Dawna Epperson is in the kitchen, cutting up fresh bananas, grapes, apples, and oranges and tossing them into large pails to make a colorful breakfast fruit salad, sprinkled with mealworms, for three very hungry and very special chimpanzees who have become her friends over the past six years. As two frisky ferrets playfully scuffle at her feet, Epperson looks up from her duties to catch a glimpse of forty-year-old Kitty peeking at her from the chimp compound just outside the kitchen window. Kitty's housemate, Lulu, blows a loud and sloppy raspberry kiss through the bars as if to say "Hurry up." The girls are so intelligent that Epperson has to keep them entertained, so she quickly pours red punch into three paper cups, walks through the door, which narrowly separates the chimp living area from the kitchen, and gently hands each one her early morning snack. Lulu, just two years younger than Kitty, holds her cup outside the metal bars, asking for a refill. Kitty reaches out her long fingers toward

Lulu Belle, a chimpanzee rescued from medical research, loves her daily sack lunch at Black Beauty Ranch. (The Fund for Animals)

Epperson as well, but holds on to a carrot, as she is famous for her attempt at bargaining for what she wants. A loud thud is heard in the enclosure next door as Midge, a powerful twenty-seven-year-old male chimpanzee, slams his foot on the ground. Lulu claps her hands—a trick to get more Kool-Aid.

It is a much different life here for all three chimps, research animals who spent most of their long lives in small cages deprived of sunlight. Midge, named Specimen ID CH-637 in his manila file folder, underwent numerous procedures at Lemsip—the Laboratory for Experimental Medicine and Surgery in Primates in Tuxedo, New York, part of New York University's Medical Center—and he had no socialization with other chimps or people before arriving here. Whenever a new person approaches Midge, he will do a charge display—a mock attack, ending with Midge slamming into the metal bars with amazing speed and awesome power. It is an unnerving performance that shakes the walls and rattles whoever is on the other side of the enclosure, but no one could blame him for being suspicious of newcomers. Lulu came from the same lab as Midge, and Kitty came from the air force's Coulston Foundation in Alamogordo, New Mexico, in what was the largest colony of captive chimps and a lab cited over the years for animal cruelty violations until it finally closed down. She had fourteen pregnancies there, including three sets of twins, but was allowed to rear only four babies. Researchers noted that she was often bent over, her floppy ears drooping forward, her eyes in an intense stare at nothing. Kitty's whole demeanor changed the day she met Nim Chimpsky, the first chimp who came to live at Black Beauty Ranch and a world-famous animal because of his ability to use sign language. The two chimps met through a mesh screen, and Nim, known to be able to gesture 125 words, made a motion toward the dividing door to say, "Hurry, hurry, open there!" Nim was part of an American Sign Language project in Oklahoma and one of the first chimps in history to learn sign language. Taken from his mother at the University of Oklahoma when he was three days old, he was raised as a human and by age nine, had learned more than 300 signs. Nim was the subject of doctoral dissertations, was on the cover of *Atlantic Monthly*, and had his smiling mug on TV, but when the sign-language experimentation was over, Nim was given to a research lab at the State University of New York to become a specimen for testing a hepatitis vaccine. Amory freed him in 1982 and brought him to the ranch, where he lived in a large enclosure with an indoor and outdoor area, a screened-in porch, and a raised loft of straw bedding for some privacy. He became one lonely chimp and so, after rescuing Nim, Amory called Coulston and found him a mate named Sally. She had been caught in Africa as an infant, and like many chimps taken from the wild, was shipped to the United States, where she was forced to walk upright, perform ballet, and ride a bicycle in a circus for twenty years until she was sold to science. Sally died in 1997 at forty-seven years old, following a stroke. Nim died three years later at twenty-six from heart failure.

Epperson remembers Nim fondly. One night many years ago, she was ready to go home and stopped by to say good night. With his primate hand outstretched, he pointed to the lights, then pointed to the open door, and clasped his two palms together, as if closing a book. Finally Nim placed his palms at rest, under his chin. He was telling her to turn out the lights and close the door, because he was going to sleep. Another winter day, Nim was enamored with Epperson's suede boots. In fact he thought they were his boots because he had been given a pair of donated leather cowboy boots that he had stashed up in his loft. Nim was very agitated, howling and clapping, pointing to her feet. All day he demanded the boots by putting the two sides of his fists together, touching them, then pointing to the boots. Epperson finally gave in and bought another pair. Nim taught the Fund staff that chimpanzees, more than any other animal at the ranch, need stimulation; now, every day Midge, Kitty, and Lulu are treated to something new: basketballs, paints, toys, traffic cones, bubbles, a radio, stuffed animals—even a session of nail polishing for the girls is worth a try to make life more interesting. Kitty will hold out her fingers one by one as Epperson dabs strawberry-red polish on each humanlike fingernail. It's called enrichment, and every animal deserves it. Janet Schubert, D.J.'s wife, pops in to tell Epperson that she tried, unsuccessfully, to give Babe the elephant an enriching Jell-O snack, but the pachyderm made a sour face and spit it out. The chimps, however, love Jell-O, especially with whipped cream on top. Midge, who possesses the power of perhaps 100 men, gingerly scoops a bit of Cool Whip off the top of his Jell-O cup, which was packed in a sack lunch along with peanut butter and jelly sandwiches and soda in a bottle with a twist-off lid. Although he has watched the girls for years successfully pop the tops off, Midge gets frustrated and gives up, opting to bite the lid. Each chimp has a unique way of eating. Lulu, for instance, takes the sandwich apart and eats the inside of the bread, leaving the crusts, while Midge just makes a mess.[6]

It is an exciting time for the chimps at the ranch, although they don't know it yet, because this summer construction began on their long-awaited, new outdoor habitat, which will include a small pond, waterfall, trees, play structures, and, best of all, a place where they can leave concrete behind and romp in the grass. Three bobcats will soon have a much larger open-air pen with a stream and underground den, thanks to a generous donor. The gibbons, too, will enjoy the addition of newly planted trees, bushes, and logs to increase their psychological and physical stimulation.

The gibbons are the most amusing animals by far, and unmistakably the first animals visitors hear at the ranch, sounding something like a firetruck siren. Sara, a white-handed gibbon, clutches her tiny baby, tucked into her soft, black belly (sometimes mamas arrive here with a surprise package). Sara was used for breeding gibbons for a research lab and all her babies were taken by researchers, but this is one she finally gets to keep. Sara lives with a male named Gilly. Just like their wild cousins in Southeast Asia, these soft, black lesser apes with white hands and white facial ring live in small family groups, led by the female who, when the mood strikes, sings her own unique family song that can be heard far and wide. In the morning, Sara will begin with a soft, high-pitched whistle that sounds like wind, but by afternoon it turns into a steady drumbeat of hoots that gather momentum until she and Gilly have worked themselves into a frenzy. Then another species of gibbons next door add their throaty tubalike horn section. Enter Val and June, the siamangs, amazingly acrobatic primates with shaggy black hair, arms that outstretch their legs, and a throat sac they can inflate like a balloon to be the noisiest of the bunch. Val and June are the busiest of the bunch, too, and don't spend much time on the ground, as they are constantly swinging on ropes and bouncing off logs or off the back of Rocky, a wallaroo who looks like a small kangaroo and, perhaps to his regret, shares their enclosure. Val came from a sanctuary in California that was breeding siamangs, an endangered species because of rainforest destruction (adults in the wild are cruelly and purposely killed, too, so humans can have baby siamangs as pets). When Val was just three days old, his mother overzealously groomed his nose—destructive behavior caused by overbreeding—and where his nose should protrude is a flat, hollow surface, but thankfully he can breathe just fine. Val was taken away and raised by humans, which is why he absolutely adores and needs several hugs a day. When Epperson walks inside the grass enclosure and before she can lock the gate, Val will swoop over, landing on top of her head. From here he makes

Sunny rests beside Cleveland Amory's memorial stone at the ranch. (Julie Hoffman Marshall)

his way into her arms and curls up like a baby. It is just the right amount of confidence-building he needs, because one second later the mischievous siamang is swinging through the air, flying, tumbling, and leaping over his human gymnasium.

At the end of a long day the tranquillity of the ranch is tangible in the soft, cool breeze and waning sun. Bobcats snooze on fur beds of vintage garments (donations to the ranch and a statement against fur coats), and a stray domestic gray tabby named Cleveland leaps over a perimeter fence to the ranch manager's house for dinner. It is also time for Abigail, a huge domestic pig, to appear, looking for her evening salad bowl. One fall evening, Friendly the burro stood in a field close to a shaded pavilion and a pair of memorial stones, one a tribute to Amory and the other the grave of his cat Polar Bear, who died in 1992 at age fifteen. Amory always believed the two of them would be together again. Amory's spirit rests here as well as all around the ranch thanks to Friendly, who went strolling with a salt shaker holding Amory's ashes tied around his neck. Amory's presence is felt here every day by ranch volunteers and staff who remember the many visits and how he enjoyed an evening of chess on the porch while the burros, huddled in groups, watched nearby. Most of all they remember how he spent every day walking the ranch, asking how the animals were feeling and reminding his people to take good care of each and every one.

6

From Goats to Tigers

"There is, in all of us, a force for good—the spark of compassion.
Unfortunately, where animals are concerned, not all of us have
had this spark ignited. I am not quite certain what it takes
to have this happen, although I am fairly certain that it
can happen from witnessing one specific act of cruelty. ...
But of one thing I am very certain—and that is
that, once a person has had this spark ignited,
it will burn forever."

—Cleveland Amory

WITH THE GRAND CANYON BURROS and multitudes of wildlife safe at Black Beauty Ranch, Amory did not take a vacation, as he knew too well that when you put out one fire, another one inevitably starts up. The US Navy was balking about the wild goats on San Clemente Island. This crescent-shaped, remote, and rugged landscape seventy miles northwest of San Diego was where, eleven months out of the year, the navy detonated bombs originating from its ships at sea. Just like the burros, the goats were being targeted for doing what goats do, and the navy had hired civilians with orders to punish every last one.

The tan and red Andalusian goat, no bigger than a housecat, first appeared on this island in the sixteenth century, transported by Spanish explorers off the Orange County coastline as a source of food for their return. The nibblers had pretty much coexisted with the navy, which took possession of San Clemente—the southernmost island of the eight California Channel Islands. The military had never complained about the goats getting in the way of its maneuvers, nor about the sheep and pigs who had been brought to the island by ranchers in the nineteenth century from the California mainland, nor about the indigenous island fox, the endangered loggerhead shrike, an endangered lizard, or the mice and feral cats who were all part of this environment. It is not entirely clear why the navy decided to practice the art of warfare against the goats specifically, having shot and trapped them since 1972 and reduced the herd from 12,000 to around 4,000. By the 1980s the navy offered a clear motive: it was now working with US Fish and Wildlife to protect endangered plants and the endangered animals who eat them, and it would do so, apparently, the only way it knew how.

Amory believed it to be a trumped-up charge and had to convince officials that there was a better way than merciless destruction. The navy ought to take the tens of thousands of dollars it would spend on contract killing and put it toward humane trapping, he said. He pulled all of his strings. Secretary of Defense Caspar Weinberger, a Harvard alum, seemed to care about animals, as he had previously stopped military researchers from shooting dogs to study their wounds. Amory reminded him that the Naval Academy mascot is, after all, a goat. He garnered support from a congresswoman,[1] he alerted the media that the navy was bullying billy goats and suggested a new recruitment slogan: "Join the Navy and shoot the goats." A navy commander in charge of the military's goat eradication program, who was not too amused, argued that no one hated goats, but that the military was just trying to follow the law. Amory wondered how anyone could think these docile animals were more destructive than exploding bombs. Four times the killing was called off at the eleventh hour, the animals won a reprieve, and Amory got the chance to try another daring rescue. Herding the animals on horseback was clearly impossible because it was one thing to send horses or burros down a river, but another to send animals off at sea. Herding on foot was not a smart choice given the island's steep ravines that dramatically plunge to the sea, and the rocky terrain covered by prickly pear and cholla, not to mention the unexploded shells. The Fund wanted to be the first in America to try a new method devised by New Zealanders involving a four-barreled gun, but not the kind that fires bullets. The latter had perfected a tool using air compression to blast a huge, nylon parachute-net to the ground and cover any running target, as big as an elephant or as small as a bird. It sounded more fancy than it appeared—like a sawed-off shotgun with a metal box attached.

Early one windy morning in summer 1983, the Fund's rescue helicopter hovered above the island as ten media helicopters swarmed into the same airspace, hoping to get exclusive coverage. First the Fund's pilot, a Canadian bush pilot named Mel Cain, had to find the animals, who blended in so naturally with the barren terrain and spanned the entire twenty-mile-long island. Once he spotted them, the chopper dove in and out, swooped and swayed in the deep, narrow canyons, sinking 500 feet to chase nannies and billies on the run. The Fund's net gunners, New Zealanders Graham Jacobs and Bill Hales, took turns aiming for one, possibly two, goats on the run. (The noise and commotion would often scatter wild pigs—animals the Fund

Cleveland Amory gets an exuberant greeting from some of the Andalusian goats he rescued from San Clemente Island. The US Navy had planned to exterminate these rare animals. (The Fund for Animals)

would later return to save—but for now it was all about goats.) Once the net was blasted, four large and heavy bolts went along with it, helping to drop the net to the ground and secure the catch on all four corners. No tranquilizers were used and not a hair on a billy goat's beard was harmed. Once the confused goat was immobilized, the helicopter touched ground to let a volunteer crew off to tie up the animal's legs and hoist the body on board. If it was too large, they would leave the goat in the net sling to dangle its way to a corral at the north end of the island.[2] Trapping and transferring goats, often one at a time, was a long and slow process. Not much time could be spent on the ground, in order to avoid live shells. No one—human or goat—was injured, but in order to gain the military's approval and have access to the most dangerous section of the island, the southern half, where most of the weapons land, the Fund had to take out a $10 million insurance and liability policy to protect the navy from any disasters. The goats ran and hid in canyons and crevices on this part of the island, and there was no way to flush them out without going in. The Fund also had to agree to pay for most of the rescue costs, which averaged $100,000. Rescued goats were put on a naval supply barge for an eighteen-hour trip to San Diego, then transported by cattle truck to adoption centers. Dozens were destined for Black Beauty Ranch.

Amory was back at work, convincing the public that, like the burros, goats would make great pets, and calling them gentle and easy to love. He knew this firsthand, having smuggled a kid into his hotel room at the Holiday Inn for show-and-tell during interviews. The adoption fee of $35 for females and $25 for males helped to offset costs. Mostly the Fund was concerned with finding good homes and making sure each goat had a companion animal waiting, or else people would have to take home two; no eating or milking of goats was allowed, or breeding, since goats had to be spayed or neutered. The Fund was besieged with calls, and people drove in from Vermont and other distant places, attracted by their sweet goat faces. The Fund's Operation Goat rescue went on for three consecutive years, one month at a time. About four thousand goats were saved and nearly all were adopted. In an ironic twist it turns out that the Andalusian goat, the one the navy was so quick to dismiss, is a genetically distinct animal, with only two hundred left in the world today. Champion breeders are champing at the bit to get one of their own. There are no more goats on San Clemente Island, but the military still uses the area for training.

Cleveland Amory, wise as an owl inside the raptor flight cage at his
Wildlife Rehabilitation Center in southern California. Most wildlife here
are injured because of conflicts with humans. (The Fund for Animals)

More recently it decided to start "controlling" the indigenous island
fox, claiming there are too many.

If not for the San Clemente goat rescue, Amory would not have met
an amazing and dedicated couple who wound up being the primary
reason why The Fund for Animals could establish its third sanctuary,
the Wildlife Rehabilitation Center, and why this facility is so success-

ful today. Chuck and Cindy Traisi had read about the impending goat slaughter in the newspaper and thought the navy's position was ridiculous, especially the scenario of a hunter shooting animals from the sky. Chuck was working for the Department of Defense as a civilian in security and was able to influence the navy, mainly because he knew lots of juicy secrets that the national media would love to hear. The couple mulled it over. They wanted to do something, but first Chuck picked up the phone and called The Fund for Animals, presenting what information he had and asking for Amory's blessing. At 1 A.M., Chuck made a call to the secretary of the navy's office and two hours later, the shooting was called off. No doubt the phone call helped, because Amory called Chuck right away to offer a hearty thanks. The Traisis figured that was the end of their role as animal rescuers, but shortly after the goat operation, they received a call from Amory, who told them he had a run-down dog-and-cat shelter in the mountains northeast of San Diego in a town called Ramona, which was donated to the Fund by an elderly woman.[3] This shelter had provided temporary refuge for dozens of Andalusian goats before they made the trip to Black Beauty Ranch, and now Amory needed someone to take charge of running it. He asked the Traisis if they would quit their jobs (she was a teacher) and dedicate their lives to saving animals. Cindy immediately assumed that Amory didn't know anyone else in the San Diego area, but soon enough she and Chuck gave notice to their employers and began planning a new life.

In 1985 the Traisis took over the Ramona shelter and the calls for help came pouring in: a coyote with a mangled leg caught in a steel-jaw trap, a golden eagle blinded and with a swollen head after being hit by a truck while eating roadkill, a malnourished raven stashed in a cage in somebody's home. It was apparent that there was a real need to transform the shelter into a state-of-the-art aid station for local wildlife in trouble because of humans. Once all the dogs and cats were adopted, Cindy enrolled in classes to learn how to rehabilitate animals for the purpose of releasing them back to the wild. The shelter grew from four to thirteen rural acres, shaded by cottonwood, honey locust, and grand oak trees, to accommodate wounded animals found by sheriff's deputies, animal control, federal wildlife officers, and neighbors who finally had someplace to take these critters and give them a second chance. Today it is typical to see upward of 300 animals being nursed back to health by five full-time staff, including the

Traisis and a veterinarian. They have successfully sent bears, cougars, and bobcats back to the forests; hawks, owls, and falcons back to the sky; and skunks, possums, and raccoons back to the woods. It is an exhilarating moment when the cage door is lifted and a healthy animal is set free. Cindy says, "Your heart pretty much goes into your throat."

Each animal is a different story, but probably the most memorable releases are the bobcats because they are so bold. Generally, with most wildlife, when the door flies open there's a blur, then the fuzzy back end of an animal growing smaller as it tears off into the distance. In

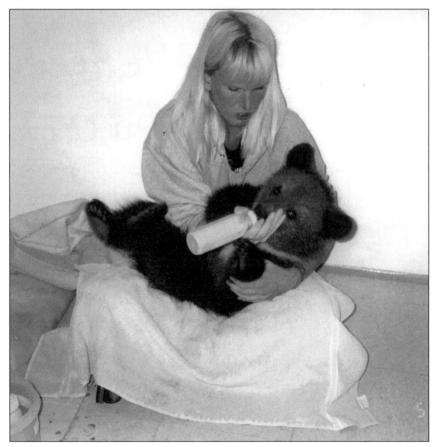

Kim D'Amico bottle feeding a rescued grizzly bear cub at the Fund's Wildlife Rehabilitation Center. Someone had illegally tried to raise the young bear as a pet. (The Fund for Animals)

Chuck Traisi releasing a healthy, rehabilitated golden eagle back to nature. (The Fund for Animals)

the case of the bobcats, however, the door opens but the critter stays inside. Remove the top of the carrier and still, the bobcat stays. This animal will stare into your eyes, growl, stick out a tongue and growl some more. Many times, a bobcat will walk backward out of the cage and, when you are very still, will take off running.

Once a rehabilitated animal is freed, there is great hope that he or she won't be heard from again, but that is not always the case. The daily work of a rehabber can be incredibly sad and frustrating. For example, there was a coyote pup, just nine days old with a bullet in him, carried by the shooter's wife, who was angry that the animal refused to die. And the baby bobcat, found dragging her body through the desert, declawed on all four paws, after being dumped, helpless to find shelter, water, or food. But for every tragedy there are victories to nourish the soul. It does not get much better than watching a raven, kept in a cage all her life, discover her wings and the wide-open skies, or a family of skunks who knew only wire and concrete get their first taste of fresh air, and the green outdoors.[4]

The past twenty years have been a mixed blessing, with the gift of great insights and lessons on the nature of animals and of humans, and how our fates are intertwined. Cindy marvels at the proud spirit and resilience of wild animals despite all that humans have done to strip them of their dignity. For instance, she will never forget responding to a call about an injured mallard on a lake and arriving to see a barbecue skewer sticking out of his throat. Some may not view Cindy's work as crucial—she's not saving a species from extinction—but she sees the morality of giving back what is due to animals who are in a bad predicament not because of nature but because of human ignorance or cruelty. It is increasingly important work, as human populations are rapidly spreading into what were once wild areas. She believes that if urban wildlife are even going to survive, it will require tolerance and appreciation of their strength, courage, and individuality—qualities that Cindy and Chuck are privy to every day. The Traisis hope to build a new hospital so they can bring their work to an even higher level and do more for more animals.

Amory visited the Traisis often and so it was sad that he was not around, at least in body if not in spirit, to see his Wildlife Rehabilita-

A rescued tiger's way of saying thank you to a Fund volunteer. (Copyright, Raymond Eubanks)

Clean water was a novelty for these tigers rescued from a fake sanctuary in Colton, California, where authorities discovered ninety dead tigers, many of them starved to death. (Copyright, Raymond Eubanks)

tion Center spearhead an unprecedented massive rescue and rehabilitation effort, costing $1 million over two years of around-the-clock diligence, for some of the greatest predators in the world. In spring 2003, California wildlife officers received an anonymous tip that a tiger cub was being held illegally in Colton, about a two-hour drive from the Fund's rehab center. Officials who went to visit the private residence could not have prepared for what they saw: a filthy compound littered with ninety dead tigers, some of whom had been tied to a car bumper and starved to death. It was impossible to walk around the home without stepping on bones, feces, or decaying calf carcasses. When the officers opened a freezer on the porch, they found themselves staring into the blank eyes of sixty-one tiger and leopard cubs. Eleven more skinny and dehydrated cubs, both tigers and leopards too young to open their eyes but still alive, were imprisoned in a dark, tiny crawl space in the attic. The rescuers were chilled to the bone, thinking how unfair it was to keep these magnificent creatures locked away from their natural world, with no excuse other than malicious cruelty to deny them food and water. This hellhole was, ironically, named Tiger Rescue, and billed itself as a retirement home

Happy tigers in their tub, which was filled for the first time by Fund volunteers. (Copyright, Raymond Eubanks)

for performing animals. The state immediately called in The Fund for Animals to take charge of these animals, some barely alive, amounting to thirty-nine tigers, twelve leopards, two African lions, a mountain lion, and four burros who were so badly treated they had to be dragged off the property because they could not walk on their overgrown hooves. The cubs, along with a couple of juvenile tigers with mange, were whisked off to the Fund's wildlife center, where Cindy and her volunteers filled their tiny bellies with formula, watching them double in size almost overnight. She then set about contacting more than 100 sanctuaries to beg for permanent homes for the many big cat refugees, and chose only reputable ones that would not exploit the animals by putting them in roadside zoos, for instance. The Exotic Feline Rescue Center of Indiana opened its doors to eight leopards, and the Rocky Mountain Wildlife Conservation Center in Colorado welcomed a mix of leopards and lions and twenty-one cubs. California's Shambala Preserve, operated by actress Tippi Hedren who starred in Alfred Hitchcock's 1963 film, *The Birds*, adopted six tiger

The Fund gave rescued tigers their first experience with toys. (Copyright, Raymond Eubanks)

cubs, while the Folsom City zoo's rescue program took in a couple of young tigers. The Austin zoo's rescue program had room for the puma. But there was still the problem of thirty-nine adult tigers in Colton, stuck in what amounted to tiger jail.

An estimated 5,000 to 10,000 tigers (20,000 big cats in all) in the United States are spending miserable lives in private homes as pets or confined in inadequate "sanctuaries." They are painfully declawed, defanged, bred, and exploited for monetary gain, and the large major-ity—90 percent—will die within two years from malnourishment and related health problems. But since tigers reproduce readily, there are many in need of rescue. That fact disgusts animal activists when they think of an endless stream of unwanted cats and dogs sitting in city shelters. While federal law bans the interstate trafficking of big cats for the pet trade, enforcement is spotty by understaffed, underfunded wildlife agencies that make enforcing hunting regulations a priority,

A relaxed tiger rubs on a log. He and the others will soon be relocated to a sanctuary with lakes and green pastures. (Copyright, Raymond Eubanks)

and states are free to accept the breeding and selling of tigers and other exotic animals, such as lions, leopards, cheetahs, jaguars, and cougars. Tiger Rescue proved that it is easy to smuggle in a tiger under the radar; the previous year, officials had seized ten neglected tigers from the same facility. It was an extreme case that alerted many people to the tragedy of the exotic pet trade. Activists claim that the solution is to teach people to stop using wild animals as pets, especially cute, cuddly cubs who can grow to be 800 pounds and snap your limb off like a toothpick. It is virtually impossible to domesticate a wild animal. In the case of tigers, people who try are forever stealing their wild-born right to freedom, because no one will be able to send them back to Asia.

The Traisis saw their job clearly: find the tigers a life with some measure of joyful wonder. With exotic cat sanctuaries full to capacity, it was apparent that a new sanctuary would need to be built. The Performing Animal Welfare Society (PAWS), which owns three sanctuaries for abused and abandoned performance animals and victims of the exotic pet trade, stepped up to build the tigers a new, ten-acre habitat at its Ark2000 site in San Andreas, northern California. The Fund for Animals shouldered the $250,000 financial burden and went to the Internet to hold online auctions with the help of celebrities. Bids were taken for autographed scripts from the TV shows *Joan of Arcadia* and *King of Queens*, as well as personal items donated by comedian Richard Pryor, actor Dennis Franz, singer Chynna Phillips, actress Anne Meara, and comedian/actor Jerry Stiller. A personal telephone call from soap stars Grant Aleksander and Julia Barr, backstage tours of *As the World Turns*, and tickets to David Letterman brought in a healthy amount of cash.

While Cindy stayed in Ramona, Chuck held on to his promise to himself and the tigers to stay at Colton and care for every one until all had made the trip to their new home. Hundreds of people volunteered to help him, but most had no tiger experience at all. Most pressing was to secure the dilapidated cages and hang tarps over them for shade. Chuck made the rules: no fingers, arms, or toes anywhere near the tigers, which was smart given that at one tiger sanctuary, a volunteer who had stuck her arm inside an enclosure for a moment to show her family how friendly the beast was lost a limb in a split second. It was okay to talk to the tigers, though, and tell them a better life was just around the corner, and Chuck did so every night. Cranky tigers lying around on concrete slabs desperately lacked amusement, so

Chuck dragged in 1,000-gallon stainless-steel tubs to cool their furry bellies. He could see how much happier they were by their chuffing—a soft sound like a train—and the contented look on their faces as they settled into the water. Sprigs of rosemary, which tigers apparently love, stirred them into a euphoric frenzy. Best of all was the abundant food that satisfied ravenous cats who could not seem to get enough to eat for the first five months. Every day, Chuck shopped for 650 pounds of flesh, usually chicken, fortunately stumbling on a restaurant supply company that offered a discount. Still, he paid $500 a day and put it on his own credit card. The job was twenty-four hours a day, and to avoid a killer commute, Chuck decided to make a hotel room home for the long haul, talking to Cindy by phone every night. Just a few months, he thought.

In the summer the next year, the first group of eight tigers made the journey to Ark2000, a place where for the first time they could roll in the dirt and sleep beneath the shade of oak and pine trees. It was amusing to watch the tentative tigers first set paws on grass, something totally unfamiliar. Soon they were trying awkwardly to run—something they could not do in their Colton confines—which turned into pouncing and leaping. The wooded hillside was heaven, with several ponds and a pool deep enough for swimming. The tigers mingled and slept at the end of the long day, finally at peace. The Fund for Animals found justice. Thanks to the Fund's and the Humane Society's attorneys, who pushed for felony charges, the owner of Tiger Rescue, John Weinhart, who had earlier been arrested for illegal breeding among numerous charges of cruelty to animals, was sentenced to two years in jail. His companion, Marla Smith, was punished with 180 days in jail. Everyone involved in the tiger rescue said it was the most rewarding job ever and thanked the Fund for stepping up to coordinate and pay for it all. Cindy is at peace, too, because Chuck is finally home.

A rescued tiger playing with his traffic cone stops to get a scratch from Fund volunteers. (Copyright, Raymond Eubanks)

7

Saving Pigeons, Stalking Hunters, and Shooing Buffalo

"One of the dangers of hunting is that hunters shoot each other. Frankly, that's something I applaud. Not a lingering death, of course, just a nice, quick one. Actually, I'd like to see 500 hunters a year killed by rabbits. That would be my favorite statistic."

—Cleveland Amory

THE 1990S WERE called the Decade of the Animal in large part because animal rights had, for the first time, merged with mainstream consciousness. No longer were individuals who spoke out for the welfare of other creatures shunned or shoved to the fringes of society. It was a good era for The Fund for Animals, with its budget of about $2 million, more than 250,000 members, and countless volunteers, and the ability to combat cruelty on numerous fronts: through litigation, legislation, education, and direct care of animals at three animal rescue facilities. For certain there were other animal organizations, such as People for the Ethical Treatment of Animals, that had more money, far better fund-raising skills, and greater memberships, but no one could outshine the Fund's leader. During this period, Amory directed his organization to make a return to its roots as a powerful force against hunters, and it did so in new and imaginative ways. The Fund enjoyed an impressive win second only to the baby seal campaign, but this time Amory rallied his troops around victims who were not so cute and fuzzy as marine mammals on the ice. Some people liked to call them "winged rats," and no one seemed to care that they, too, feel pain and deserve respect for their unique and rightful place on earth.

The situation was similar to the Bunny Bop, as the hunters Amory met had a mob-style bloodlust, but in this case for pigeons. The Fred Coleman Memorial Labor Day Pigeon Shoot, a macabre celebration of death, was the pride and joy of Hegins, a small farming and coal town forty miles northeast of Harrisburg in the heart of Pennsylvania Dutch country. The festivities began at 7:30 A.M., as shooters who had paid $78 took their spots in a large grassy field, about thirty yards from a white box stuffed with two dozen pigeons sitting on a springboard, waiting for the ceremonious call: "Pull!" One yank on a string and these living, breathing targets were catapulted sky-high. All of this happened before a cheering crowd packed into Little League bleachers, eating hot dogs and guzzling beer while pointing, yelling, and generally having a good ol' time. The ultimate goal for the shooters was a trophy and $500, along with any side bets of the day.

The Fund for Animals had always been bombarded with calls from people enraged about such outrageous stunts, demanding that Amory do something about it. But to actually be present at the pigeon hunt, to hold a dying animal and see this disrespect for life, was what ultimately solidified Heidi Prescott's commitment to the cause. Prescott, the Fund's national director at the time and a former student of Edinboro State College in Pennsylvania, felt a special obligation to protect animals in this state, particularly the pigeon, also known as the rock dove and the international symbol of peace. That the Hegins shoot was being taught to children as morally acceptable made it something the Fund had to stop. The killing had been going on since 1933, the year a town committee decided that blasting birds into oblivion would be a good way to raise money for the community. Live pigeon shoots actually predate Hegins, going back to the 1800s in Europe, where it was considered a sport for the upper classes. Its counterpart in modern America was anything but classy. By 1990, Hegins had grown into the world's largest pigeon-killing field (yes, there were others), attracting 250 shooters each year. A local brochure touted the shoot as one of the "few activities left in the country where families can gather together and enjoy a pleasant day of fellowship in the outdoors." Prescott, Amory, and plenty of Fund volunteers saw quite a different story: 6,000 pigeons had to be hauled into Hegins by the truckload, and they were anything but fair game. Brought in from out-of-state breeders and gathered by gun clubs from other towns, many of these birds had never flown or spread their wings, and had been deprived of food and water for days. In their dehydrated, weakened state, when the box was sprung open, most of them could barely waddle outside. Some perched atop the box, blinking in the sun, while those who managed to take flight did not get much farther than six feet into the air when they were blasted into a flurry of feathers. Within seconds, pigeon bodies toppled to the ground, wings flapping and bodies flopping.

Before The Fund for Animals caught wind of Pennsylvania's dirty secret, local humane officers had been trying to make a case for stopping the shoot but without much success, and so activists decided it was time for direct action. Some dashed onto the field to take a stab at releasing birds from their cages. When successful, their courage was rewarded with a charge of theft, and if activists dared set foot within the thirty-five-foot, fenced circle of the shooting grounds, they were slapped with a trespassing charge as well. Once the birds were released, at least outside the circle, they were anyone's fair game. One activist scaled a pizza stand to reach a disoriented pigeon. After another bird landed in a tree over the crowd and minutes later fell to the ground, vomiting blood but still conscious, the crowd laughed and pointed while a child kicked the still-twitching body. Another injured bird flew past the spectators and landed underneath a car. Fund volunteer Vicki Stevens attempted to approach the vehicle nonchalantly, but was stopped by a man with a smug, toothless grin who asked if she was looking for something. Bursting with the desire to reply that yes, she was looking for his brains, she turned her attention to the wounded victim, managing to pull the bird out from under the car. The heartbeat was strong. With the pigeon gripping her fingers, Stevens made the long walk through the taunting crowd to the Fund's mobile veterinary hospital in the parking lot. Along the way she noticed a man and a woman wearing T-shirts with the slogan "There's the law, and then there's the Order," adorned with the drawing of a hooded Klansman carrying an Uzi. Another man wore a hat that read "Save Our Military" and pictured two male stick figures engaged in anal intercourse in a red circle with a red slash through it. And all this at a so-called family event.

Into the shooters' circle, after the last shell exploded, came the "Trapper Boys," eight- to twelve-year-old local kids whose job was to finish the job. The remaining pigeons struggled to evade capture, but to no avail. The boys collected them roughly, grabbing many by a wing, clutching three or four at a time and swinging them by their feet like a lasso. Some of the boys threw the bodies like a football; others slammed their catch to the ground. Sometimes they took hold of a live body and wrung its neck or yanked off the head. Half-dead pigeons were randomly pitched into fifty-five-gallon barrels to suffocate among a mounting pile of birds. A Fund volunteer noticed that a small group of birds had gathered outside a small fence and were being ignored by the children. Interestingly, one bird seemed to be trying to help the others, hopping over and preening their wings. While the shooters were taking a lunch break, the children noticed the group and ran out to kill them. The helping bird managed to make it to a tree, while the boys collected a few of his companions, but when the children left, the helper returned to the remaining birds. The cycle repeated again until all the birds were gone. When the Trapper Boys were done, Prescott and many Fund volunteers scoured the fields and woods along the perimeter for any sign of life. As a certified wildlife rehabilitation expert, Prescott would stabilize the birds. Once, when she turned a pigeon over, she saw that both legs had been blown off, and the bird was doing the "gaspy thing" they do just before they die—and this one was clearly going to die. At that moment she made a silent promise to do everything she could to stop this insanity. For her efforts, Prescott and her companions were arrested and she served fifteen days in county jail. Incarceration was well worth it, as was watching the birds she had managed to save fly over the fields.

Early on it became clear that no one in the small township was going to give any ground in what became a massive culture clash. Those who supported the shoot boasted that it raised about $40,000 for parks, the local fire department, and the community at large. Just like those who justify killing animals for fur, meat, entertainment, or research, Hegins's leaders defended their practice because, they said, it was legal. But what is legal is not necessarily moral—public lynchings, for instance, were once legal. The Fund offered to buy them state-of-the-art clay pigeons and trapshooting equipment. The answer was a resounding no. The Fund then offered them $15,000 to cancel the shoot. No deal. An anonymous person offered $70,000 to stop the shoot. Still the town dug in its heels. Robert Tobash, the event's main organizer, defended the shoot by claiming that no one in Hegins hated pigeons. "We treat them well—until they get shot." The shooters called it a great sport that gets into your blood. An elderly woman who came every year with a folding lawn chair, shared the sentiment

The Humane Society's Wayne Pacelle joins the protest of Pennsylvania's pigeon shoot.
(The Fund for Animals)

that the animals deserved it because they serve no purpose and have no rights. Amory defended the birds, having watched pigeons in Central Park respond positively to people who were kind to them. Pigeons are smart, as historians know from the important role they played in carrying messages in World War I. Amory warned the people of Hegins about the Fund's persistence and vowed to stay and fight forever. The day he turned seventy-four, he was right there, leading about 1,000 activists, some from Europe, who protested with bullhorns and banners amid a deafening crowd of 10,000 spectators ("… a hell of a way to spend your birthday," he said). The protest evolved over the years to take on different tactics, often out of frustration. Activists handcuffed themselves to canisters filled with concrete and sat down on Route 25, the main road into town, to block traffic, stealing a half day from shooters while authorities had to cut through the blocks of concrete.

The law, at least on the books, appeared to be on the side of the pigeons. According to Pennsylvania's Crimes Code, it is illegal to shoot, maim, or kill a homing pigeon. The Fund documented several cases of pigeons with leg bands who were being shot, and was able to trace many of the bands to individuals in Maryland, New Jersey, New York, Pennsylvania, and Virginia who had hand-raised the birds as racing and homing pigeons. But still, state troopers made no arrests. The same Crimes Code also states that one may not abuse or neglect "any animal." Evidence mounted as the Fund documented abuses each year: in 1994, of about 5,500 birds released, nearly 3,500 were not killed but wounded and later collected by Trapper Boys. A few were dead before the trap door opened and hundreds were never accounted for, having fallen outside the fenced park. Schuylkill County judges must use a different sort of dictionary to define abuse, because despite documentation and a four-inch stack of affidavits, a county court judge failed to allow Pennsylvania humane officers to enforce the state's anti-cruelty laws and sue the town committee that sponsored the shoot. The Fund searched for every loophole, even trying to get the state agriculture department to stop the shoot based on its rule that importing birds across state lines is illegal if they have an infectious disease. Veterinarians had determined that many of the shot pigeons had salmonella and chlamydia. In signed affidavits, animal doctors claimed that these diseases spread rapidly to birds and possibly to humans, and as birds came into Hegins by the truckload—with fifty stuffed into each small crate—it was very likely that disease had spread. This argument never went very far, and the Fund soon focused on legislation. There was a clear sign of trouble with one lawmaker, US representative Timothy Holden, former Schuylkill County sheriff, who said he was more than glad to enjoy the shoot rather than legislate against it. It was a long, ugly battle before the state legislature as lawmakers refused to hear bills or hastily voted them down. A succession of governors, too, refused to intercede. Governor Tom Ridge called the shoot a sport and a local issue, although at the time there were laws overseeing dogfighting and other spectator "sports." No one, it seemed, gave a damn about pigeons. These birds, like the maligned prairie dogs of the West, often fall into the same category—as rodent pests. They are neither pets, nor wildlife, at least according to bureaucrats, so they fall into cracks where they are ably denigrated. The result is that lawmakers allow anyone to do what they want to these animals. They are shot, trapped, drowned—you name it—and no one lifts a finger.

Amory was determined to fight until he won. Hegins became a high-priority campaign, so much so that it dictated where the Fund's next

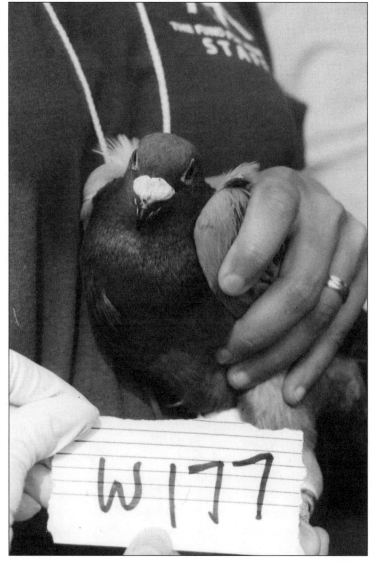

One of the few survivors of the annual Hegins pigeon shoot. Stopping the shoot was one of the Fund's greatest wins. (The Fund for Animals)

annual convention would be held—in Harrisburg, the state's capital, to draw attention to the protest. Reporters joked that the local Marriott was so inundated with activists that it changed its menu of meat and chicken to soy burgers and tofu. As the Hegins shoot was on the national radar, numbers swelled and people on both sides became more vocal and more ugly. Protestors sported signs with the words "Big Guns, Small Minds," while spectators countered with "Save a Pigeon, Shoot a Protestor." Now spectators were getting into the fray, grabbing for downed birds before the rescuers could, teasing and tormenting them by dangling the birds by a wing and out of arm's reach. A young teen was charged with disorderly conduct for pelting protestors with a dead pigeon. Smoke bombs, fistfights, and bizarre and disturbing images—such as shoot supporters parading with pigeon heads atop picnic forks, stole the national spotlight. The highlight by far was the "Pigeon Chomper," nineteen-year-old Scott Bradley, who was caught on videotape picking up a live pigeon, squeezing it, and then putting it in his mouth as the crowd cheered him on. He shook the bird in his mouth before biting its head off and then mounted it on his glasses. The Fund put out an alert with a $500 award, and someone called to report that Bradley lived in the nearby town of Minersville. The Pigeon Chomper was arrested for disorderly conduct and fined $150.

The Fund for Animals had had enough, and decided to focus solely on what had seemed to get lost in the media hoopla: the pigeons. Through its mobile veterinary hospital, called the Wounded Birds First Aid Station, it saved several hundred birds with the aid of volunteer medical workers who gave them sugar and fluids in the hope of transferring them to rehabilitation facilities on Chesapeake Bay. The Fund never did, however, give up documenting the shoot with video and photography for the long legal battle. It ran negative ads with graphic displays of garbage cans filled with pigeon carcasses. Amory called for a state boycott on tourism, just as many social movements have done in the past, sending his volunteers out to distribute leaflets about the shoot to motorists at rest stops throughout the state. The Fund held showings of a thirty-minute video documentary by a Washington, D.C., filmmaker, Eddie Becker, called *Gun Blast: Culture Clash*, which was nominated for several independent film awards.[1] It was a momentous day when Hollywood joined the battle. The Fund compiled twenty-seven certificates signed by famous actors, including Alicia Silverstone and Dennis Leary. Alec Baldwin wrote a letter to

Governor Ridge saying, "This event is a slaughter and an embarrassment to your state. Animal rights activists, many of whom are members of the movie industry with an eye toward producing films in your state, are optimistic that you will take the necessary steps." The Fund found support and coverage from the *Washington Post, USA Today, People* magazine, *CNN*, and Jay Leno, who threw in some jibes during his monologue. Pennsylvania was under siege. Amory took Pennsylvania to task by calling its governor a heartless, gutless person who was bringing shame on his state.

In 1999 the Labor Day committee in Hegins voluntarily canceled the shoot. It would be nice to say that the town leaders came to their senses, but that was not the case. The state supreme court ruled in a landmark decision that a lower court two years earlier had wrongly told an SPCA humane officer that he could not apply the state's anti-cruelty laws to the sponsors of the pigeon shoot. In a unanimous decision, the high court stated that the officer could indeed seek a court order to stop the shoot. In essence, the lower court had erred in telling the officer that he had no jurisdiction in Schuylkill County because he hailed from Philadelphia. Therefore, in order to stave off a lawsuit and an expensive court battle, Hegins caved. For the first time in sixty-five years, the grassy fields of Hegins's town park would be quiet come Labor Day. The ruling was a monumental win for Prescott, in particular, and for The Fund for Animals, because justices zeroed in on the issue of cruelty, devoting two of eleven pages to the pain and suffering of the victims. Writing the opinion for a unanimous ruling was Chief Justice John P. Flaherty, who called the shoot cruel and moronic: "Hundreds of the pigeons suffer a slow and painful death and eventually die from their wounds or starvation. An additional two thousand or more are not given any sustenance, drink, or veterinary care and suffer pain until they are eventually killed." The justices noted that the methods of the Trapper Boys were contrary to the accepted veterinary methods of euthanasia and caused the birds additional pain and suffering.

Prescott was thrilled, but her only regret was that Amory did not live one more year to see the end of his crusade in Pennsylvania. Town reaction was predictable. Shoot organizer Tobash said the cancellation was his idea because he was not willing to subject the townspeople to "additional violence and terrorism by a group of out-of-state individuals who feel they are morally superior to our local citizens." Citizens lamented the loss, and some wrote letters to the local paper calling it a blow to tradition, to family fun, and to good, churchgoing people. One year later, shoot organizers and opponents agreed to a settlement banning pigeon shoots altogether by order of the Court of Common Pleas of Schuylkill County. A domino effect followed, with more states, such as California, abandoning their tradition of live pigeon shoots. Texas and Arizona are the notable holdouts, still allowing such activities to go on. The end of the Hegins shoot was not the end for the state of Pennsylvania, however. There are still contests that allow the blasting of live pigeons for money and prizes.

The battle in Pennsylvania revealed some themes that took on even greater importance in hindsight. That Hegins's adults supported children taking part in the killing was indeed significant, given that studies at Yale and institutes of higher learning have shown that kids who abuse animals are more likely to commit violence against humans. The FBI and the American Psychiatric Association have reported that cruel acts against animals are a red flag signaling future violence. This has been the case in the ruthless and violent school shootings around the nation from the 1990s to the present, in which youths who shot down classmates and teachers have a shared history of cruelty to animals. Dylan Klebold and Eric Harris, who gunned down classmates at Columbine High School in Colorado, bragged to their friends about mutilating animals. Luke Woodham, who shot and killed classmates two years ago in Mississippi, wrote in his journal about how he beat, burned, and tortured his dog. The Fund noted that in six years of thirteen random school shootings, twenty-seven people were killed and fifty were wounded by kids living in areas where hunting is a way of life. They used the same high-powered weapons they had used to kill animals; they knew how to hide and wait for their prey and had no qualms about killing defenseless beings. Some even wore camouflage hunting jackets the day of their killing spree and had placed telescopic sights on their deer-hunting rifles, which they had stolen from their fathers or uncles.

Another theme was the hope that ethical hunters would speak up and condemn a shoot that was not truly a hunt. A few hunters did raise their voices to say that hunting is not a spectator sport and to deride the townsfolk for taking such pleasure in killing. But the Fund wanted a greater, more spirited chorus. It hoped to hear hunters condemn prize-winning contests that are based on a body count, to hear them say that using tame birds as live targets is not a sport but a butchering, and killing for the sake of killing. There is a clear and easy distinction between killing for meat that will be eaten and killing for pure enjoyment, which is what led the media at large to stand beside the activists. As one outdoors writer put it, Hegins was like an open boil on the sport of hunting precisely because the shooters were labeling themselves as hunters. But the voice of the ethical hunter remained largely silent out of fear that any attempt to ban a hunt would lead to banning all hunting, and so there seemed little room to argue about morality.

In the middle of the Hegins campaign, Prescott had made a valiant attempt to make allies over the bad apples—the ones who give all hunters a bad name—by attending the national gathering of hunters at the Fourth Annual Governor's Symposium on North America's Hunting Heritage. The traveling conference, sort of a state-of-the-state affair, is a way for like-minded souls to get together and build strategies for promoting sport hunting to the general public. In 1995 the conference was in Green Bay, Wisconsin, and Prescott was scheduled as a speaker and the sole voice of an animal activist. The invitation arrived after she had attended the book signing of a man who had written about cleaning up the image of hunting. She had asked him to sign a petition stating that sportsmen are opposed to pigeon shoots because they violate the rules of fair chase. He would not lift a pen, so Prescott stood on her soapbox, explaining the fact that while hunters like him would talk about such things, they wouldn't do anything about it, which is why they lose credibility. Apparently she was heard. A huge controversy erupted when hunters learned that The Fund for Animals would be appearing at the symposium. There were boycotts, but to the credit of the organizers, Wisconsin's Department of Natural Resources, they did not back down. Prescott's speech was well attended, perhaps out of mere curiosity from all the hype, attracting 400 people in a line that backed out the door. She told the crowd that yes, she is anti-hunting and they are pro-hunting, but that they should put differences aside and talk about working together against events that give their kind a black eye, such as coyote- and prairie dog-killing contests. There are plenty of ethical issues that divide hunters, for instance the use of bait to lure deer to an area where a hunter perched in a tree stand can shoot them at point-blank range, the use of hounds fitted with radio collars to scare a mountain lion into a tree, and the acceptance of hunting bears, squirrels, mountain lions, and mourning doves during the months when the mothers hunt or forage for food to nurse their young. Hunters, then, are a large part of the reason why young babies are left alone to die in the nest or in the den from starvation. Since hunters claim that many unethical activities are practiced only by a minority of hunters, it makes sense that ethical hunters ought to be able to control their own—or at least try. Prescott pointed out that anytime those outside the hunting fraternity speak against some aspect of killing animals, outdoors writers go into a tizzy, writing hysterical pieces wholeheartedly supported by the industry. During the pigeon-shoot campaign, it was the National Rifle Association, the Unified Sportsmen of Pennsylvania, and the state's Federation of Sportsmen's Clubs that fought her group tooth and nail in the legislature and in the courts. Sometimes hunters are their own worst enemy.

Prescott was rated the symposium's third most popular speaker. Her words had summoned an unusual detente; some hunters came up to thank her for coming. A man from the state Fish and Wildlife Department told her it was the first time that compassion for animals had been addressed at the conference. As a frontline soldier in Amory's ever-growing Army of the Kind, Prescott was fearless, and her reputation as a leader in animal protection flourished. During the Hegins fiasco, the tall, attractive blonde had been shoved, hit, body-slammed against a car, and in the hallowed halls of the state capitol, some lawmakers had even pretended to shoot rifles at her. Prescott likely inherited her sense of justice from her father, a Methodist minister. At the age of eight, she was horrified to see a circus offering live chameleons tied to pins as living jewelry. She paid the $1 per pin, which quickly used up her allowance, and whisked the wriggling creatures back to nature. She remembers first hearing Amory on television talking about seal hunting. In her childhood fantasy, she became a wizard who could wave a magic wand and stop the killing. But it was not until college and shortly after her husband brought home a live woodpecker he had found in the street, that Prescott realized she wanted to dedicate herself to helping animals. She attended a conference where Wayne Pacelle, the Fund's executive director at the time, spoke about stalking hunters in the field in the name of protecting animals. Soon she was organizing an excursion into the woods to protest hunting and, true to form, Amory was introducing Prescott as his new Washington, D.C., coordinator.

The Fund for Animals made famous the idea of confronting hunters in the forest. Amory sent his field agents to the fields—literally—to find ways to obstruct death. One cold day in November, the opening day of deer-hunting season, Prescott waltzed into a hunting area in Maryland's McKee Beshers Wildlife Management Area, a state park along the Potomac River. There she followed a hunter into the woods and rustled a pile of leaves with her feet. Some time later, a wildlife officer arrested her. Prescott, then twenty-eight years old, made this statement at her hearing: "I did not physically strike, obstruct, yell at or insult any of the hunters with whom I communicated. I simply exercised my First Amendment right to voice my objections to the cruelties of sport hunting and to walk on public lands." After refusing to pay the $500 fine, she was taken away in handcuffs and stripsearched, according to the *Washington Post*, then sent to a maximum-security jail for fifteen days (two off for good behavior). Prescott found it funny when Amory yelled at her while she was incarcerated. For some reason he thought she was on a hunger strike, but she wasn't—the jailers just wouldn't serve vegetarian food unless it was for the sake of religion or diet. Amory visited often, and yelled often, to make sure she ate. Whenever she got the chance to make a phone call, she called him and he'd yell at her some more; she found it sweet that he cared so much. Prescott finally persuaded the warden to give her vegetarian meals as a matter of ethics, and without much to do besides eat, she visited the library and, for the first time—she was embarrassed to say—had the chance to read *The Cat Who Came for Christmas*. Hearing Amory's voice through his writing gave her much-needed comfort. Essentially Prescott was sent to jail for approaching a man and saying, "Good morning. Can we go talk over coffee instead of killing an animal today?" She would be jailed at least a dozen more times, in various states, for hunter harassment—impeding the hunt was illegal—and was the first animal rights activist to be jailed under such a law in the United States. Because of her willingness to go to jail and gain public attention, a long and lively debate ensued in the media and in the courts over the right to hunt versus the right to free speech. The Fund for Animals, then, was the first to make a serious legal challenge of so-called hunter harassment laws.

The term "hunter harassment law" originated with an incident in spring 1990, involving an activist trying to save a bison in Yellowstone National Park. John Lilburn of Missoula, Montana, was standing fifteen feet away from a hunter who was aiming at a bison feeding at a lake outside the park when Lilburn stepped in front of the rifle and yelled, "Don't shoot!" A wildlife officer shoved Lilburn into a tree and the bison was shot. The incident set off a war between hunters and protestors in dozens of states over who owns the woods and the fate of wildlife. A Montana district judge ruled that the law under which the activist was charged was too broad and vague and flew in the face of free speech. The judge said that it prohibited one type of speech (anti-hunting) but not the other (pro-hunting), and thus went too far to regulate expression by one particular group over another. But the decision was overturned a year later by the Montana Supreme Court, which ruled that the safety of hunters in the field outweighed any potential free speech concerns. Soon new hunter harassment laws popped up in dozens of states, with challenges offering sometimes conflicting and confusing rulings.

Activists kept going into the fields (with bail money stashed in their pockets just in case), calling it a "Hunters' Education Outreach program." They blew whistles and clarinet mouthpieces and banged on pots and pans; some donned Day-Glo orange vests with the words "Don't Kill Me, Too." They went after deer hunters in Hell, Michigan, and trudged through swampy marshes in the town of Alabama, New York, where ducks were the targets. Prescott even once trailed former president Bill Clinton while holding a sign to protest his duck hunt. In addition, activists sought bear hunters in Promised Land, Pennsylvania. But most saboteurs turned their attention to deer hunting, particularly bow hunting, because they saw it as the most cruel.[2] It became their calling to follow the hunters and say things like "But you don't need to hunt" or "You don't have to eat deer," and "Deer feel pain and suffer." Fund activists went out in groups, generally from two to six at a time, and the majority were women, although Markarian, Pacelle, and other men joined in, too. Most often the tactic was small talk to scare off animals. Amazingly, there were very few violent encounters, although one New York hunter fired three shots above an activist's head. Another hunter struck Markarian with the butt of his rifle and threatened to kill him. Markarian was just sixteen years old when he joined Prescott at his first hunt protest. On her orders he stood in the parking area guarding cars from vandalism.

It appeared as though Amory's Hunt-the-Hunters Hunt Club was taking shape. It was an interesting time, as activists and hunters who converged in the remote woods had day jobs as librarians, lawyers, construction workers, street sweepers, mechanics—you name it. As one was followed by the other, in and out of the brush, soon both sides were learning a lot about the other. The question that usually sparked a lively conversation was "Why do you kill?" Killing, the hunters argued, was their "God-given right." Some admitted it was a "macho thing." One man who had bagged a 336-pound female bear smiled at his human shadow and said "It felt great." Prescott had seen a poll at the national hunting symposium revealing that the vast majority of hunters—85 percent—kill for "fun," and now she knew it was true. Animal activists were not the only ones who found it odd that in a democratic, pluralistic society, some state legislatures were saying that activists were not to carry on these conversations with hunters who were engaged in hunting. One syndicated columnist observed, "You can shoot an arrow into a deer's eyeball. That's legal. It is *illegal* to speak the words: 'I don't think you should shoot that arrow into a deer's eyeball.' " What would or would not remain legal continued to be an issue, as hunter harassment laws in Connecticut and Wisconsin were struck down as unconstitutional while laws in Maine, Massachusetts, and Montana were challenged. Federal judges in Connecticut said that protecting hunters from conduct by those opposed to hunting was not a compelling state interest.

Meanwhile the NRA, along with the Congressional Sportsmen's Caucus,[3] joined the court battles by taking out advertisements in outdoors magazines urging hunters not to talk to anti-hunting activists. The latter were delighted that they were being taken seriously, and stressed that it is a privilege to hunt, not a right, and that the animals are in an unfair fight against bows and arrows, rifles, and handguns, not to mention high-tech homing equipment and bait. Wildlife has a hard enough time in the woods with natural predators, Amory said, so let them be, or at least let the animal protectors be there. That would not be the case, because the entrenched power of pro-hunting politics prevailed with a law sponsored by a Montana senator tucked into a crime bill package, making it a federal crime to be in the woods scaring off animals and talking to hunters. The Fund for Animals had fought with all its heart, but the hunting lobby, including the Wildlife Legislative Fund of America, was a powerful voice speaking for what had become a multibillion-dollar business that fed itself by promoting such mantras as "Hunting is a great American tradition."

Although hunter harassment laws would stay on the books, they would no longer affect the Fund's activities. Stalking hunters was, in the beginning, a fantastic way for Amory's people to ratchet up the national hunting debate a notch or two, but once hunting became a topic of conversation at the dinner table and anti-hunting became a mainstream ideology,[4] it was no longer necessary to confront individuals in the woods. The anti-hunting movement had evolved, and Amory and his Fund for Animals now turned to other channels of social reform, countering pro-hunting messages in schools,[5] and reaching out to people through articles and opinion pieces that asked a growing urban population to consider more than one side of the story. Yes, hunting is an American tradition, Amory wrote. It is a tradition of killing, crippling, and ecological destruction and one that has wiped out species and brought others, such as the bison and grizzly bear, to the brink of extinction for the sake of human recreation. It was a tradition of faraway kingdoms centuries ago, where animals were slaughtered for pure entertainment. The Fund encouraged people to at least stop and think before accepting as truth such rationalizations of killing as "Humans must hunt to save animals from overpopulation or starvation." On the millions of acres of public lands where no hunting is allowed, one can see healthy, thriving wildlife. Wake up, Amory said, to the fact that wildlife agencies are purposefully manipulating herds and increasing numbers to satisfy their main constituencies, hunters. In some states, agencies had mandated the need to kill more bucks than does in order to allow more fawns. They burned forests to create game habitat and added supplemental feed to produce enough numbers for their hunting license lotteries. The popular shoot-to-save argument was mostly reserved for deer—the hunter's popular target—and yet, according to numbers compiled by the Fund with data from federal and state wildlife agencies, deer represented less than 1.5 percent of the 200 million animals hunters slaughtered every year, a list that includes 50 million mourning doves, 31 million rabbits, 27 million squirrels, 25 million quail, 20 million pheasants, 13 million ducks, 6 million grouse, and 4 million geese, as well as 120,000 pronghorn antelope, 100,000 elk, 25,000 black bear, 1,500 mountain lions, and 1,100 brown and grizzly bears. Then there are moose, bighorn sheep, bobcats, mountain goats, ordinary goats, wolves, foxes, cranes, crows, coots, turkeys, javelinas, raccoons, woodchucks, and coyotes.

To learn how hunting got its stranglehold on wildlife management, one must to go back to the early 1900s, when passenger pigeons,[6] and other animals being hunted to extinction, spurred new laws. President Theodore Roosevelt, a hunter, and conservationist Aldo Leopold helped build wildlife refuges where the hunt could continue. Hunters invested their dollars in habitat and live targets with licenses and fees, and the federal government seemed to be on the road to becoming a game rancher. In 1937 it established the Federal Aid in Wildlife Restoration Act, also called the Pittman-Robertson Act, which imposed an 11 percent excise tax on rifles, shotguns, and ammunition. (Congress amended the law in 1970 to add a 10 percent excise tax on archery and handguns.) These funds were set up to be funneled through the US Fish and Wildlife Service, an agency of the US Department of the Interior, and given to state wildlife agencies, and were used mainly to build shooting ranges, promote hunter education, and for other purposes that served their primary constituency: hunters. Eventually commissions were established to oversee state agencies, but were immediately and heavily dominated by individuals interested in seeing wildlife dead, namely hunters, ranchers, and farmers. So while the majority of the population does not hunt, the minority—13 million or 6 percent of the population—makes the rules about where the money goes and how it is spent, turning government institutions into de facto hunting, trapping, and fishing clubs. Having hunters oversee wildlife, Amory said, is like having Dracula guard the blood bank. Hunters countered that they pay for habitat and so it makes sense that they should receive the lion's share and make the rules. Actually, there are more gun owners than there are hunters, so not everyone who contributes to Pittman-Robertson funds necessarily expects to be provided with hunting grounds. Though it is the majority—66 million people—who enjoy wildlife activities that do not include killing—such as photography, hiking, and birdwatching—and who spend double (about $40 billion) what hunters spend annually on recreational appurtenances, such activities are still not at the forefront of management priorities. Meanwhile, the US Supreme Court has determined that wildlife is to be held in trust for all citizens, no matter what their hobbies.

None of this, however, was quite as bad as what the federal government did in the 1990s under the name Animal Damage Control.[7] Professional hunters hired through this program, under the US Department of Agriculture, killed any animal that might compete with agricultural interests—crops or cattle. Hunters trapped, poisoned, shot from aircraft, chased down, or burned out of their dens millions of birds and hundreds of thousands of coyotes, beavers, skunks, raccoons, bears, mountain lions, badgers, foxes, bobcats, and, inadvertently, many dogs and cats annually, costing taxpayers tens of millions of dollars. Our government poisoned eagles, killed all but a handful of mountain lions east of Texas and the Rocky Mountains and almost wiped out grizzly bears and wolves in the lower forty-eight states. One employee was so disgusted with what his agency was doing to wildlife, particularly mountain lions, that he stacked eleven severed heads of lions killed by government workers in a pyramid beneath a tree and snapped a photograph of it.[8]

In spite of this pernicious activity sanctioned at the federal level, in the late 1990s, wildlife agencies in many states experienced a monumental shift toward managing wildlife for diverse interests, thanks in large part to the growing desire of citizens to treat animals more humanely. When agencies refused to abandon cruel methods such as the steel-jaw leghold trap, people responded with ballot initiatives to make them do so. Who controls wildlife? became the overarching question for underfunded and overtaxed wildlife managers caught in the middle. Who should they listen to: the hunter, angler, rancher, politician, or average citizen? Missing in that equation, of course, was the voice of the animals. The Fund took the lead on many welfare campaigns, coordinating with other grassroots pro-wildlife groups around the nation. In 1992 it drafted and promoted a ballot initiative passed by more than 70 percent of Colorado voters to stop the use of bait and hounds in hunting. Today it is also no longer acceptable in that state to hunt bears in the spring—a time when cubs are dependent on their mothers, and hunters may not use smelly goods to lure mother bears into a trap, an act that biologists say trains bears to link humans with food, and ultimately to their own demise when they become "problem bears." Nor is it legal to send packs of radio-collared dogs into the woods after the bruins. Soon after this legislation was enacted, Wyoming, a state that once allowed hunters to use spoiled food and dead dogs, cats, beavers, lambs, and even horses as bait, instituted a similar ban, but only for one year and in limited areas. In 1994, voters approved a Fund-backed ballot initiative to forbid the use of bait and hounds to hunt bears and cougars in Oregon, and another to end all commercial trapping on public lands in Arizona. Two years later, in order to win a ban on mountain lion hunting in California (which succeeded by 2.5 million votes), the Fund helped place $25,000 worth of radio ads featuring Robert Redford on the air. Local pro-wildlife organizations claimed the Fund played a crucial role in the anti-hunting law. Most important, it was the first time the NRA had ever lost a large-scale hunting referendum.

That same year, Amory directed his organization to put its energy into the fight against steel-jaw leghold traps, devices that inflict prolonged pain and suffering on wildlife. A coyote caught in such a trap might run in circles, dislocate a joint, and eventually gnaw off its foot in a wrestle for release. These traps are known to be indiscriminate killers that also catch nontargeted species, such as pets. One of Amory's favorite cats, an orange tabby named Peg, limped her way onto the porch at Black Beauty Ranch's guesthouse and into his heart. A trap was clenched around her mangled paw. The leg had to go, but the sweet-natured feline spent a long, peaceful life at the Texas sanctuary. The Fund also joined grassroots coalitions to pass statewide ballot initiatives banning leghold, as well as body-gripping traps in Arizona, Colorado, and Massachusetts. In Montana, where the cattle industry ran roughshod over wildlife, humane reform was sorely needed but certainly not welcomed. As one rancher put it, "I don't think you ever, ever want to get in a fight with agriculture in Montana." Amory never did pick easy fights, and so while his people were in Hegins hell, the Fund locked horns with Montana and the feds over hunting buffalo at Yellowstone National Park. The buffalo campaign was the second high-profile, highly significant campaign of the decade, one that Amory did not see come to an end in his lifetime, but because of his resilient workers, particularly Schubert, the Fund did enjoy some moments of glory and helped to keep the momentum going in the right direction. Unlike the pigeon shoot—a win that bolstered Amory's belief that hunting would ultimately come to an end—the battle over buffalo proved that the overall war would be hard-won, because in Montana, men proved they could be just as ruthless with a species that embodies our cultural heritage, freedom, and the American West.

The story of the American buffalo, also called bison, is a national tragedy like no other. The shaggy behemoths once ran in great numbers across the mountains and open plains—an early explorer noted a single herd that was sixty miles long and twenty miles wide. Then came the great massacre of the 1800s. The US Army waged its vile campaign against the Native Americans and the sacred animals who provided a wealth of spiritual life. *National Geographic* reported that the US Congress was so threatened by the Great Plains Indians, it wanted to annihilate the one animal they relied on for food, shelter, and clothing. The killing continued with William "Buffalo Bill" Cody, who was hired by the Union Pacific Railroad to kill thousands of buffalo each year to feed the rail workers. In the 1860s, buffalo were shot by average citizens from the comfort of railroad cars. By 1880 a mere 200 animals were left, seeking refuge in Yellowstone National Park, which was established in 1872 as a safe haven of impenetrable land. But poachers were relentless, and left unchecked, by 1902 the herd was down to 23 animals. Once the Park Service and its rangers were established in 1916, however, the population rebounded. Today's Yellowstone buffalo are the direct descendants of the wild, free-roaming herds of North America that were nearly eclipsed by government-sanctioned killing. They truly are the last of the great herds that are able to roam unfettered as part of a wondrous ecosystem that provides food for recovering wolves, coyotes, grizzly bears, raptors, and other creatures that flourish within and beyond the park sanctuary. Every other herd outside Yellowstone is isolated in fenced pastures, managed like cattle for food. The buffalo itself is a national treasure. Its distinctive image is the insignia of the Department of the Interior and the emblem on park ranger uniforms. And the designer of the nickel said he could think of no image more emblematic of America. All of these are reasons why their history of slaughter, abuse, harassment, and disrespect at the hands of those who are supposed to protect them is unimaginable, and why the buffalo became a major focus for Amory. To him the buffalo symbolized all of the injustice done to animals.

The modern nightmare goes back to the winter of 1989, when cold-hearted and ignorant hunters brutally slaughtered 569 buffalo whose only crime was roaming outside the northern boundary of the park in search of food. The kill was sanctioned by ranchers, Montana lawmakers, and federal agriculture bureaucrats who had decided they would not tolerate buffalos near cattle grazing on leased public lands adjacent to the park, because buffalo can carry a bacteria called brucellosis, which can cause their own kind to abort fetuses. For two decades, scientists and biologists have argued that there is no real risk to cattle—there has never been a documented transference of the dis-

Bison peacefully grazing at Yellowstone National Park. Outraged by the government's needless slaughter of these docile animals, Cleveland Amory dubbed bison the national symbol for all the injustice done to animals. (D. J. Schubert, The Fund for Animals)

ease from buffalo to cow—but the cattle industry and its supporters have vehemently refused to accept any risk, no matter how minute. The disease is spread through body fluids, such as when an animal licks the afterbirth of a calf or attempts to breed with an infected buffalo. Neither scenario is at all likely because cattle don't breed with buffalo, and since buffalo head back to the park in spring, they are long gone by the time cattle are grazing.[9] But in 1989 the state of Montana was fuming that the National Park Service couldn't keep "its" buffalo—about 3,200—inside the park. Annual migration is in the buffalo's blood. In winter, when grass within the park is limited, something tells these magnificent creatures that it's time to amass at the northern and western boundaries and head out. Buffalo don't know about fences or boundaries: their ancestors once roamed from Canada to Mexico, from the Rocky Mountains to Washington, D.C. As the Yellowstone buffalo set out on their journey, they were shot at close range like sitting ducks—or rather like parked trucks, since one buffalo can weigh up to 2,500 pounds. The spectacle of blood spilling on the falling snow in Yellowstone's pristine wilderness was too much for animal rights groups to bear, as well as for the general public who felt that no one should countenance such barbarity to protect cattle from a phantom disease. Tourists on snowshoes, snapping photographic memories, were horrified to see the buffalo they believe are an asset to the park experience gunned down in front of their eyes. Witnesses saw pregnant bison cows being shot and the bodies of their aborted fetuses lying in the snow. One bison was gutted while still alive, pawing the earth as a knife slit a gash up its belly and the hunter's party and the outfitters laughed. A *Boston Globe* reporter witnessed a fourteen-year-old boy squeeze the trigger and watch as the animal tried to get up no less than forty times in five minutes, blood spilling from its nostrils. A Montana Fish and Game warden told the young hunter to get closer and fire two more shots, and finally it was over. Newspaper editorials called the spectacle a firing squad more than a hunt, as docile buffalo tumbled to the snow in groups of twenty at a time as they followed the ghosts of their ancestors. Buffalo would periodically stop to munch grass beneath the snow, unconcerned about the humans nearby—they were used to tourists and their cameras—as someone aimed a rifle and turned the snow bloody red. TV crews captured buffalo that took as long as thirty minutes to die; calves were shot beside their mothers. The slaughter made headlines across the nation and was condemned by everyone, it seemed, except by what Amory liked to call "slob hunters," as well as the state of Montana and cattle interests. The hunt continued the following year, with hunters aided by park rangers and Montana's game wardens. Calves were trapped and sold at auction. It was time for the activists to come out.

D. J. Schubert, twenty-seven years old, had flown in from Washington, D.C., to protest the buffalo slaughter. If ever there was a hard-working and sagacious animal rights activist in Amory's Army of the Kind, it was Schubert. He will work so late that he winds up sleeping on the office floor, rising the next morning to continue the project. A political lobbyist and a wildlife biologist, he knew something about the scare tactics the cattle industry was willing to promote in the name of competition to cattle grazing. With Amory's blessing, he traveled to Montana for hands-on work on behalf of the most beleaguered beast, and took part in making history as one of the first people to disrupt the buffalo slaughter. It proved to be one of the most rewarding and frustrating times for Schubert, who first heard of Amory when he graduated from college in 1983. Dismayed with his work as a biologist because the job was more about politics than about protecting habitat, he learned that The Fund for Animals needed someone in its Washington, D.C., office to help build political pressure on behalf of animals. Schubert ended up helping start the Fund's Silver Spring, Maryland office, which eventually would take over most of the campaign work from the New York headquarters. From there he would head to Texas to manage Black Beauty Ranch with his wife, Janet, an elementary schoolteacher who worked for Amory on children's programs and literature, including the Fund's teen magazine, *Animal Free Press*. Janet became involved in animal activism at the age of thirteen, when she sent in her first $2 to the Fund's seal campaign. Once drafted into the Army of the Kind, she remembers attending one of Amory's book signings, during which Amory, knowing she had a good voice, spontaneously asked her to belt out an a capella chorus of the Carpenters' song, "Bless the Beasts and the Children." Amory loved this song from the 1972 film by the same name, in which six troubled teens at an Arizona summer camp wander off and stumble across a herd of buffalo. The teens devise a scheme to liberate the animals that are about to be slaughtered.

The morning of March 13, 1990, the sky was still dark when Schubert rounded up a handful of activists from Missoula on rented snow-

mobiles, on skis, or on foot, and went to Yellowstone's western border to monitor the bison and see if they could chase them back into
the park. At Horse Butte, a few miles outside the park, they came
upon eighteen bison peacefully grazing near an ice-covered lake. The
animals were slowly lumbering along in single file at the edge of the
lake during a big snowstorm that was hampering their efforts. The
hunters arrived on snowmobiles, accompanied by Montana wildlife
officers and an NBC News crew. Schubert and his friends took to following the herd and shouting to spook them away from the hunting
party. For the next several hours it was pure chaos. Activists chased
after the hunters, trying to get in front of the line of fire of a rolling
Block .45-70, the same gun used to massacre buffalo a century before.
They tried to grab the keys and yank them out of the ignition before
the shooters could maneuver for a better angle. When a bison cow
and her calf broke from the confused herd, one of the hunters blasted
away. He beamed, holding his rifle up to the media: "A heart shot."
The cow tried to get up, her frantic calf running in circles. One of the
activists jabbed the shooter in the chest with a ski pole and told him
to put the animal out of her misery, which he refused until one of his
own suggested that he do so. When a protestor cried over the second
shot bison, a game warden mocked her grief by kneeling down beside
her and pretending to cry. Then a third bullet whizzed by John Lilburn who had tried unsuccessfully to get in the way of the shot and
would later end up in court charged with hunter harassment.

The winter of 1991, Schubert was back in Yellowstone, keeping a
close eye on groups of buffalo near the border inside the park. His
objective was to walk behind them pushing them farther back into the
park. Hazing was against federal law, and officials had warned Schubert, so he went in at night. A friend drove him to the park on a
cloudless night with a full moon that lit the way and revealed the
rounded shapes on the horizon. The bison were shocked to see something with two legs at nighttime and took off in a stampede, heading
deep into the park. Schubert regretted that the animals had depleted
some of their precious energy, but over the course of two weeks of
doing the same drill, the animals got used to it. It became a sort of
dance: the bison would form two lines making a backward V, with
Schubert in the lead. It was something to marvel at, but the leader had
to pay close attention to ensure that the buffalo didn't run him over
and to watch for rangers who were looking for him, hoping to slap

him with the charge of harassing wildlife. Of course, if he were shooting a bullet into a buffalo, that would be okay by Montana's ethics and laws.

The last night of this activity was a memorable one. It was dark, about 7 P.M., and a group of bison had already left the park. The goal was to pitch snowballs in their general direction to get them to safety before sunrise. The trouble was, there was not enough snow on the ground, so Schubert decided he would throw rocks near, not at, the buffalo for the same effect. Rocks across the river were the perfect size. With his pockets loaded down, and bundled in four layers of winter clothing, heavy socks, and rubber boots, Schubert walked up to the riverbank, searching for a shallow spot to cross back over the swiftly running water. Halfway there, his boot hit some slippery moss and into the river he went. He did the sidestroke, until he could grab hold of something and pull himself out, the whole time fully aware that this was how some people died. A rock that was well secured on the riverbank did the trick, and he managed to stand up, then noticed that his pants were completely frozen, like ice cubes stuck to his legs. Dragging his cold, stiff body like Frankenstein, it was a long walk back to his friend's house to call his wife, and when he finally stopped shivering, to have a good laugh.

The Fund would remain in Montana for the long haul, with Schubert returning again and again to keep herding—saving up to 150 animals in a good week—and other activists videotaping and documenting events for the public and for the courts, as the Fund became the first group to file a lawsuit to end the slaughter. At least six more lawsuits would follow, and half would be won. In January 1991, when Schubert was out hazing his herd and getting his feet wet, so to speak, the Fund received its first legal blow in a federal district court in Helena. Judge Charles Lovell ruled, "Hunting is a time-honored avocation and a legitimate and recognized method of animal control." A Montana rancher who supported the ruling was quoted in the newspaper, saying that "only through management by man can the park be kept in a natural state." He was the kind of person who, Amory would say, couldn't be dumber if you cut his head off. Because of the public outcry over video footage and the pressure on lawmakers, though, Montana's legislature gave in and banned the use of outside hunters. Now the guns were in the hands of Yellowstone National Park rangers and Montana Fish, Wildlife and Parks Department game wardens.

Amory and Schubert were furious. None of it made any sense. Elk, which outnumber buffalo ten to one, carry brucellosis and migrate outside the park onto cattle grazing lands, but the state of Montana had never made an issue out of this, probably because it makes money from selling elk hunting licenses. Why not vaccinate the cattle? Why not look into nonlethal methods, such as putting some of the responsibility on ranchers to adjust grazing times? The state could purchase additional pastures to allow room for the buffalo to roam. It was clearly interested in only one final solution: kill the entire herd. After all, when the first 569 buffalo were slaughtered, no one bothered to take tissue samples to determine if the animals were actually infected with the disease. And the killing was indiscriminate: males and buffalo too young to give birth were killed just as were pregnant females, despite the fact that only infected pregnant females might, theoretically, transmit disease.

The first win was small but meaningful, and it came in spring 1991, when the Fund got an injunction by a federal court in Washington, D.C., to stop the killing of twenty-five buffalo slated for research. Three late-term, pregnant buffalo had already been killed five miles north of Old Faithful, their bodies partially skinned and cut open by biologists who collected samples of internal organs and body fluids and bagged their fetuses. The judge upheld an 1894 law stating that rangers are there to protect, not destroy, native wildlife in Yellowstone, the only exceptions being to protect human life and to benefit animals inside the park. It seemed that the buffalo would be spared their final indignity: being studied to death. But that would not be the case for long. Two years after the ruling, a US Department of Agriculture–funded study at Texas A&M University involved rounding up late-term, pregnant buffalo inside the park and shipping them out of state for observation. The Fund sued, claiming that bureaucrats failed to complete an environmental review of their plan to purposely infect the buffalo with brucellosis and watch to see if they aborted. A federal judge temporarily halted the project. The worst news came in 1996 when, as a result of a court settlement won by Montana on behalf of its cattle ranchers, the Park Service signed the Interagency Bison Management Plan, by which buffalo would be lured with hay outside the park into holding pens and tested for disease. If they tested positive or pregnant, they were sent to the slaughterhouse. If negative, they also were sent to slaughter. Those that tried to escape were executed on-site by livestock agents with high-powered rifles. Many of these buffalo were at first captured inside the park. Every day they were rounded up, then shot, regardless of their age or gender. The Fund, joined by environmental groups such as the Sierra Club, lost its challenge in federal court. A whopping 1,100 bison outside the park were killed in 1996, for a total of more than 2,300 killed in the previous seven years.

As activists braced themselves for another round of buffalo games for winter 1997, a new threat loomed on the horizon. The weather proved to be the worst in a long time. Heavy snowfall and impenetrable layers of ice kept the buffalo from the grass they needed to fatten up their bodies and grow shaggy winter coats. Soon the beasts were gathering on the park borders. Emergency hearings were called because it looked as if buffalo were on the brink of collapse. Amory and Montana's congressman Ron Marlenee slugged it out on the floor. "Mr. Amory, did you or did you not say that Montana hunters would shoot their mothers if she was on four legs?" Amory gleefully responded: "No, Mr. Marlenee, I was misquoted. I said the Montana Fish, Wildlife and Parks Department would shoot their mothers if she was on four legs, and they did not include that I also said in many cases, I had reason to believe that she was." All sides by now were pitted against one another. Montana governor Marc Racicot lashed out at the National Park Service and Superintendent Michael Finley for refusing to feed the buffalo in the park and failing to keep the wild animals contained as if in a zoo. The Park Service refused to stop grooming trails, which give the herds an attractive, snowpacked route out of the park. Things were getting desperate when the governor suggested a fence, but the Park Service said it would not bode well for migrating elk and deer, not to mention that it would alter the very nature of Yellowstone as a wildlife refuge. Racicot appealed to President Clinton and the Department of the Interior to step in because this wildlife issue was being controlled by agricultural interests. To make matters worse for the buffalo, the state legislature was able to ensure that its Department of Livestock had taken control of buffalo away from Montana's wildlife agency. Now butchered buffalo meat was being auctioned off with proceeds going to the state. Five buffalo grossed $102,000, and heads sold for $260 each.[10] The process of turning wildlife into domestic cattle was complete, and those in power had undone years of progress in the conservation movement.

If one group bears responsibility for the largest slaughter of wild American bison since the great kill-off of the nineteenth century, it is APHIS—the US Animal and Plant Health Inspection Service—a little known department and an arm of the US Department of Agriculture, which incidentally also operates Animal Damage Control. APHIS was now pressuring Montana cattle ranchers by saying it would yank the state's brucellosis-free status and require expensive tests of cattle if the "bison problem" did not go away. APHIS had a zero-tolerance policy and was maneuvering to make sure that cattle interests maintained control of buffalo. Brucellosis was now a political disease.

Among the people directly affected by all the political wrangling were some cattle ranchers who were appalled at what was going on in and around the park. One said that he did not agree with the killing and took measures to vaccinate his cattle against brucellosis. Everyone who played a role in trapping, shooting, corralling, shipping, or slaughtering the buffalo tried to explain it by pointing at someone else. By spring 1997, when the Yellowstone buffalo should have been frolicking carefree with their newborn, a total of 2,500 buffalo were dead, more than 750 that year alone (the highest death count since 1975), and the rest of the herd looked sick. Emaciated buffalo were gnawing on pine bark, which biologists call starvation food, and Montana lawmakers were calling for a new hunt, not because the herd was suffering but because state senator Tom Keating was worried that his livestock workers were overtired from pulling the trigger. US senator Max Baucus suggested that the buffalo in the park be "managed a little more." While the political rancor continued, the Fund stayed focused on the cruelty, capturing images of a buffalo kicking for three minutes after being shot in the head, hung upside down, and having its throat slit. The Department of Livestock was excessively cruel during its roundup and transport of buffalo, allowing panicked animals to hurt one another. Videotapes showed broken horns, bloody cuts, and animals with their eyes gouged out. From the slaughterhouse were haunting images reminiscent of the days when the army ravaged the species to spite the sacred bond between buffalos and Native Americans. While the bloodshed continued, scientists pointed out that agribusiness would never be able to get rid of brucellosis in the wild, for it is carried by bears, wolves, and coyotes. The Fund called for a state boycott, taking out a $24,000 advertisement in *USA Today*, that read, "The state of Montana has zero tolerance for buffalo, so we need you to have zero tolerance for Montana." Amory urged the public to write Montana's governor and refuse to spend one dime in his state until he grew a conscience. People around the nation responded by writing letters to the editor published in Montana newspapers. One woman wrote in the *Bozeman Daily Chronicle*: "I wonder about the values of the people who are condoning this sort of act. It certainly makes me question how the sick and homeless are treated in your state."

By the year Amory died, close to 3,000 buffalo had been slaughtered. The National Park Service and the state of Montana drafted an environmental impact statement, agreeing to fifteen years of public hunting, continued capture and slaughter, and even quarantine facilities in the park. It took eight years to devise a plan to degrade wild buffalo to the point that they were wearing metal eartags and peroxide stripes to designate which animals were infected. The National Wildlife Federation and the InterTribal Bison Cooperative, a coalition of forty-five Native American tribes in eighteen states, came up with an alternative plan that was ignored. It would have placed a professional wildlife manager in control over wild herds, instead of the state veterinarian, and allowed buffalo to safely move outside the park onto expanded winter rangelands. Its supporters included 48,000 out of 67,000 polled by the Park Service who said that they opposed killing as a management tool, and believed the park had done a weak job of accounting for the impacts of slaughter on animals and plants that rely on the buffalo. Meanwhile, no burden was placed on cattle ranchers, as tax dollars continued to allow low grazing fees. The Fund argued as it had before: that the Park Service was endowed with the awesome responsibility of conserving wildlife on national park land for future generations, not of appeasing ranchers.

After Amory died, there was a bright spot of hope when Congressmen Maurice Hinchey, a Democrat from New York, and Charles Bass, a Republican from New Hampshire, introduced a law that would have placed a moratorium on the hazing, capture, and killing of Yellowstone buffalo on federal lands until a sound compromise with ranchers could be reached. Called the Yellowstone Buffalo Preservation Act, it would have given buffalo free range north and west of the park, granted sole control of the buffalo to the National Park Service, created a land exchange so that a small private cattle herd no longer grazed near wildlife habitat, and created incentives for ranchers to allow the coexistence of wild animals and grazing cattle. The bipartisan bill was narrowly defeated in the House of Representatives.

The awesome power of Mother Nature blessed the dwindling buffalo of Yellowstone in the new millennium. By 2003 the population had climbed to 4,000. As history is apt to repeat itself, Montana's legislature and its Fish, Wildlife and Parks Commission decided it was high time for another event to appease ranchers and set aside a 23,000-acre area east of Gardiner, north of the park border, for the hunt. The first week of January 2005, just days before the shooting was to begin, Governor Brian Schweitzer called it off, saying that he did not want a black-eye hunt to tarnish the reputation of his fair state. "I don't think we should have the equivalent of shooting refrigerators," he told the media. Or at least, he said, not until buffalo have established a greater range. Hunters and ranchers balked, saying their state was weak and cursing their governor for caving to animal rights activists; state lawmakers agreed. It appeared that the new governor was an ally of the buffalo, but that would not be the case, as he announced a new plan in the new millennium: to run every last buffalo in the park through a quarantine facility to be tested for brucellosis. As winter approached, Montana wildlife officials chose fifty people through a lottery system to carry out the first public buffalo hunt in more than a decade.

Every day, Schubert is reminded of the Yellowstone buffalo, especially when he is out feeding the animals at Black Beauty Ranch and comes across a buffalo named One-eyed Jack, who likes to sleep under the shade of a big oak tree. Schubert believes that it will probably take a cure of brucellosis in cattle to end this madness, but no one is looking for one. Or maybe it will take a lawsuit, or putting the buffalo on the Endangered Species List. There is no slam dunk. What's necessary is an overwhelming outcry from citizens to stop the killing of these noble, invaluable beings who represent everything we cherish.

8

Marching Onward

"Cleveland Amory does not have just one person to carry on his dream. His greatest legacy is that he has millions of people working in their own lives to make the world a better place for animals."
—Michael Markarian, President of The Fund for Animals

THE NEW MILLENNIUM brought a brand new day for the Animal Rights movement. On January 1, 2005, The Fund for Animals officially united with the Humane Society of the United States. Together they make up the largest and wealthiest animal protection entity in the nation and the world. Board members from both organizations had voted unanimously for the union, and Marian Probst is certain it is something Amory would have wanted. He would have been thrilled to see Wayne Pacelle and Michael Markarian—both of whom learned how to be effective animal welfare advocates by working closely with him and following his lead—now working side by side under the same umbrella organization. Amory always believed that the key to a healthy movement is teaching the younger generation to pick up the baton and take it forward. The Fund for Animals has, in a way, come full circle. Amory, of course, was a Humane Society board member. And it was Pacelle, who Amory had hoped would someday become the Fund's president, who now oversees both groups under the Humane Society banner, as well as a virtual army of animal activists including 400 paid staff, not to mention countless volunteers and nearly 9 million (1 in 40 Americans) members who proudly contribute to their campaigns.

Both the Fund and Humane Society still exist as separate organizations, but as part of their coordinated effort, they have created a new nonprofit called the Humane Society Legislative Fund—a lobbying arm that protects animals through public policy, including new state and federal laws as well as ballot initiatives. The backbone of its work is called the Humane Action Network, a free, weekly e-mail subscription service that goes out to 85,000 members, managed jointly by the Fund and the Humane Society, to notify them of important campaigns and encourage them to speak out and influence their representatives in government. The Humane Society Legislative Fund also has an Animal Protection Litigation section, driven by seven full-time, in-house attorneys—no small feat for the Fund, which once had to contract with outside lawyers—and headed by Jonathan Lovvorn, a professor of animal law at George Washington University Law School. The legal section oversees the dockets of both the Fund and the Humane Society, covering state and federal litigation involving a huge range of species, such as whales, dolphins, manatees, wolves, bears, migratory birds, farm animals, performing animals, and research animals. The alliance will no doubt help level the field in the war over how society should treat animals, considering that the NRA, for instance, spends seventeen times more on political activity than the Fund and the Humane Society combined. Powerful pro-hunting groups, such as Safari Club International, outspend animal rights groups by the millions. It is also likely that the enemies of animal protectionists will organize. Upon learning of the merger, the U.S. Sportsmen's Alliance released a statement calling it a "wake-up call" to hunters and encouraging preparation for a "powerful attack … from this monstrous anti-hunting group." The nation could be on the verge of a new, soon-to-be-defined battle over who speaks for animals.

In addition to the changes in political strategy, the Fund has assumed responsibility of six hands-on animal care facilities, combining its own three with those of the Humane Society: the Cape Wildlife Center, a wildlife rehabilitation center in Cape Cod that cares for 1,400 injured, sick, or orphaned wild animals each year; a low-cost Spay and Neuter Clinic and Animal Wellness Center in Dallas; and Rural Area Veterinary Services, a mobile unit that serves poor communities, including the Appalachian Mountains and Indian reservations, with free veterinary care.

Pacelle and Markarian had talked about this merger for months in discussing how to do more for animals. Under the new deal, Markarian splits his time between the Humane Society's office in Gaithersburg, Maryland, and the Fund's campaign headquarters in Washington, D.C. In summer 2004 the Fund moved out of its small, cramped offices in downtown Silver Spring, Maryland, into a historic rowhouse in the nation's capital. A three-story corner building erected in 1914, it was Woodrow Wilson's campaign office when he ran for reelection. More recently it served as Senator John Kerry's headquarters during his 2004 presidential campaign. The Fund was torn, Markarian jokes, because it wanted to move in during the primary and the only way to do so would be if Kerry, much more liberal than Bush on animal issues, lost. With enough office space for forty staff, the rowhouse serves as the government affairs office of the Humane Society and the lobbying arm of the Fund. Most of the new joint animal rights organization works on the huge campus in Gaithersburg, near Washington, D.C. Just as he has two commutes, Markarian has

Fund president Michael Markarian in fall 2004 speaks out against Maryland's first bear hunt in fifty-one years. The first bear killed was a small nine-month-old cub, which did not help the public image of hunters. (The Fund for Animals)

two roles. He'll remain Fund president and at the same time head the lobbying arm as executive vice president of the Humane Society.

Although the Animal Rights movement has a long history of turf wars, that is not the case here. Ever since Pacelle first hired Markarian at the Fund in 1993, before Pacelle went to the Humane Society a year later, the two have enjoyed both a friendship and a work relationship. Together they played a crucial role in ending cockfighting in three states, in banning steel-jaw leghold traps in five states, and in passing the first state law that frees pregnant pigs from life in metal crates. In a way, Markarian and Pacelle are two peas in a pod, as they are both young, highly articulate intellectuals who came into the movement intrigued by a vegetarian lifestyle. Both possess an uncanny ability to persuade others through the written and spoken word, and both upon first introduction, seem quiet and unassuming, even unemotional— something rare among activists. But make no mistake: they are intensely driven by the desire to find justice. Markarian's motivation may stem from the fact that his great-grandfather escaped genocide in Armenia. Although each was comfortable as a leader of one group, they could also see the greater benefits of a union. The Fund's staff members no longer have to take on three jobs at once now that they have a much larger infrastructure, including an investigative office to gather the facts, a litigation department to sue, and experts in government affairs to effect long-term change. A press office is icing on the cake, as field agents no longer have to write their own press releases. But it's not one-sided. The Fund brings renewed energy to a large organization that can sometimes get bogged down in bureaucratic details. The Humane Society has been infused with a nimble, hard-hitting, grassroots energy. Together they have the necessary ingredients for an aggressive agenda, but with mainstream appeal—which is the ultimate goal. As Markarian says, it's a whole new day in the Animal Rights movement, and Amory would be proud because he never had enough money to do all he wanted to do.

Staying true to Amory's mission, Markarian and Pacelle have dedicated a new campaigns section to four primary interests: fur, hunting, factory farming, and malicious animal cruelty. Fur has made a resurgence in the fashion world, as runway models like supermodel Naomi Campbell, who once swore they would never touch fur, have done an about-face. Jennifer Lopez has been seen wearing fur, as has Cindy Crawford. Fashion magazines boldly display images of fur jackets, but the big push now is fur trim on parkas, hats, gloves, and everything from handbags and boots to raincoats. Dyed purple, yellow, blue, or orange, it screams out cool fashion for bohemian youth. Fur trim has consumers asking is it fake or not? Any item retailing for less than $150 does not have to be labeled, nor do importers have to declare any of their goods under that price. According to the International Fur Trade Federation, 40 million animals are killed every year for fur fashion: rabbit, raccoon, beaver, bobcat, mink, coyote, fox, badger, ermine, fisher, lynx, marten, muskrat, otter, sable, and even wolf. That number does not include animals trapped in the wild. The steel-jaw leghold trap is still the most common trap used in the United States for animals who will become clothing. The majority of animals killed for fashion, however, are born and kept at the many fur farms in Wisconsin, Minnesota, Pennsylvania, and New York. Videotape from inside shows a row of foxes—animals who enjoy digging—stuffed into small wire-mesh cages, spinning in place, desperate for an out. No laws regulate the manner in which these animals are killed, but those who raise them prefer such methods as anal and genital electrocution by which electricity stuns the body, but not the brain, causing a massive heart attack while the animal is awake. Fur-farmed animals may be gassed, their necks broken, or poisoned by injection.[1] It is the consumer, those in the fur fashion industry say, who ultimately will decide whether fur will continue to be a viable product in the American retail marketplace. Animal advocates are keeping pace in a new age of sophisticated marketing. As a result of focus groups, it has become clear that there is no one-size-fits-all approach to convincing potential wearers that fur is cruel. Teens, for instance, thought photographs of foxes and bobcats were cute, but were not moved by images of mink, raccoons, and chinchillas and categorized them as rodent pests. To reach a younger generation, activists created an animated, short musical for their website featuring a creature called the "Furfanu," similar to Dr. Seuss's tree-saving Lorax, who guides a cartoon female shopper into the world of fur farming so she can see exactly what goes into making her fur coat. Online visitors may forward the clip to their friends (it's called viral marketing) and the site has had tens of thousands of hits. Also using the Internet as a powerful tool, Markarian's staff created three domains called NeimanCarcass.net, NeimanCarcass.org, and NeimanCarcass.com, all parodies of the Dallas-based Neiman Marcus, a nationwide chain of forty-nine upscale department stores that sell a great deal of fur. Neiman's owners filed suit, trying to shut the sites down, but a judge ruled that no reasonable person could be confused by the satire. Animal advocates chose to create the first paid, antifur TV advertisement with images of the daily life of animals at fur factories and a voice asking consumers to "make compassion the new fashion." The ad was recently shown on major cable networks, including CNN, MTV, Oxygen, and Lifetime, during prime time in large markets such as Boston, Chicago, Philadelphia, and New York City. Another ad, featuring Wendie Malick of the TV show *Just Shoot Me*, has been published in the *New York Times Magazine* and *The New Yorker*, in student newspapers, and as posters on college campuses. In fall 2005, the Fund and the Humane Society launched a series of full-page advertisements in *People* magazine to spread the message that "animals need their fur more than we do." Top fashion magazines, however, refuse to print paid copy that speaks for animals.

The fur fashion industry gives Canada an excuse to continue killing and exporting baby harp seal skins, as top designers, such as Prada and Versace, turn them into garments, which is why animal advocates have made the seals one of their most prominent campaigns. The slaughter of both harp seals and hooded seals begins every year in November and continues through May, but the largest kills still take place in the spring, in the Gulf of St. Lawrence near the Magdalen Islands, and on the Front, the open Atlantic northeast of the Newfoundland and Labrador coasts. The hunters are fishermen and French-speakers who reside in the Magdalen Islands in Quebec and Newfoundlanders who kill seals during the off-season. Smaller-scale hunts are conducted by Danes and Greenlanders in Greenland and Iceland, and by Norwegians in the White Sea of Norway. Russians hunt seals in the Caspian Sea.[2] Norway remains the single largest importer of seal fur from the Canadian hunt, largely processed by one private company, GC Rieber and Sons. Denmark is a close second and sells seal furs in its stores. Italy is the largest single exporter of apparel made from seal fur, sending its products throughout Europe and Asia. Russia is also a major player in the world market for seal products, as are several countries in eastern Europe, notably Poland, Estonia, the Czech Republic, Romania, and Croatia. Add to the mix Greece, Germany, France, Spain, the UK, Belgium, Finland, and Turkey, which all have portions of the trade in seal furs. Germany and France appear to be the most actively involved in a wide range of products, reportedly experimenting with a seal pepperoni sausage and promoting seal oil as a healthy alternative to vegetable oils. Asian countries too, including China, Japan, and South Korea, import seal fur and oil. Seal penises have long been a valued item, marketed as an aphrodisiac and processed—no joke—in the town of Dildo, Newfoundland.

The numbers of seals being killed are staggering, far exceeding those when Amory first intervened. In 2003, Canada officially raised the quota and allowed sealers to club, shoot, and stab more than 1 million seals over the next three years. In spring 2006, another 350,000 or more will be killed, and once again they will be the babies. Canada's rule is that hunters may kill when the coat begins to molt and turn silvery gray, which happens about twelve days after birth. These are pups, barely one foot long, who lie at the edge of the water still not old enough to swim, eat, or move quickly. Hunters want young ones, which are more likely to have unscarred, pristine pelts that will fetch a good price in a growing skin market, which has reached an all-time high at $75 each. The large majority (a documented 96 percent) that die are between twelve days and twelve weeks old, and the process is just as cruel as in the past, if not worse. The job has become more personal to club-wielding fishermen, who are angered by Canada's moratorium on codfishing after cod stocks collapsed off eastern Canada in 1992; they blame the seals because the government-backed fishing industry tells them to.

Today Atlantic codfish populations are less than 1 percent of their pre-Columbian levels. The Canadian government and the codfish industry have consistently blamed the seals—predators of cod—for depleting fish stock and hampering its recovery. A closer investigation, however, reveals that cod make up only 3 percent of the seals' diet, and that seals eat squid, a predator of cod, which means that the food chain and the marine ecosystem are a little more complex than some would have us believe. Historically, both seal and cod populations have flourished together. There are no subtleties to how seal hunt supporters feel about these pinnipeds. A former fisheries minister who spoke before Newfoundland's legislature said that he would like to see "all of the seals killed and sold, or destroyed and burned." The government has backed that sentiment in recent years with the gift of subsidies through interest-free loans and grants to seal processing plants and their workers. While Canada has set the mechanism for large-scale massacre in motion, animal welfare advocates and scientists claim that seals are scapegoats, pointing to huge modern-day factory trawlers as the cause of overfishing of cod.

Scientist David Lavigne and his associates at the International Marine Mammal Association in Guelph, Ontario, are dedicated to understanding the seal-and-cod controversy. Their published research and reports indicate that there is no scientific evidence to support the contention that harp seals are impeding the recovery of cod stocks. They point out that nearly 100 scientists from fifteen countries signed a petition that reads, "all scientific efforts to find an effect of seal predation on Canadian groundfish stocks have failed to show any impact." Even the Canadian Department of Fisheries and Oceans' own seal specialist has acknowledged that there is no scientific basis for blaming the seals, and that his department was getting "a lot of flack" for saying so. While the government talks about the need to recover fish, Lavigne and other scientists are concerned about the effect that raised quotas and the lust for killing will have on the seal populations. Canadian writer and naturalist Farley Mowat estimates that for every dead seal counted—an average of 350,000 every year—another is shot and lost under the ice. Many are plowed over by sealing vessels, or, in the case of newborns, who cannot yet swim, they fall into the water and drown or fall victim to the ever-shifting ice floes. Add to this equation poor ice conditions, which scientists attribute to global climate change. Thinning ice means fewer pups, since seals prefer rough, hummocky ice at least twenty-five centimeters thick for breeding. Even if the ice is good, adult seals must first migrate 5,000 miles between Greenland and Canada to give birth to just one pup. Canada's quota seems unreasonable when the science does not justify the need and the seal population is almost certainly declining; the 2005 population is between 1.8 million and 5 million, depending on who is doing the survey. It's not a hunt or a harvest, but a culling of the seal herds, and truly the single largest mass slaughter of a mammalian wildlife species in the world.

After the Humane Society and The Fund for Animals both failed in their appeals to Canadian leaders to stop the cruelty, volunteer crews returned to the ice floes in 2005 to document the killing and raise greater awareness worldwide. According to a 2000 poll commissioned by the Canadian government, seven in ten citizens say they are not very familiar or not at all familiar with issues surrounding the seal

It is still legal to kill young seals who cannot yet swim, as long as their coats begin to turn spotted gray, on average around twelve days old. (Kathy Milani, the Humane Society of the United States)

hunt. Ignorance is even greater in the United States. The first day of the 2005 hunt, activists working as equal partners with Watson and his Sea Shepherd Conservation Society launched a new element to their campaign, calling for a boycott of Canadian seafood. According to the Canadian government, two-thirds of its catch is exported to the United States, yielding $2.8 billion annually for the country's economy. Natural foods giants Whole Foods and Wild Oats; Downeast Seafood, a purchaser for more than 250 restaurants nationwide; Legal Sea Foods restaurants; Spectrum Organics; Kimpton hotels and restaurants; Reel Fresh Fish Company in the United States; Marks and Spencer in Britain; plus many prominent restaurants in New York, San Francisco, and elsewhere, have all signed on to halt their purchases, particularly snow crab, Canada's largest export, until the government stops the slaughter. Those businesses that join the campaign display a colorful sticker of a harp seal with flippers up and the slogan "We Save Seals by Not Buying Canadian," donated by Berkeley Breathed, creator of the comic strip, *Bloom County*. In addition, more than 120,000 individuals have signed the Humane Society's online pledge not to buy Canadian seafood. Unfortunately, Red Lobster, the top US seafood restaurant chain, with more than 600 restaurants, and its multibillion-dollar parent company, the Darden Group, which purchases millions of dollars' worth of Canadian seafood each year, refuse to join the boycott.

Paul Watson, his wife Allison Lance-Watson, and their crew of volunteers also made the journey back to the ice in spring 2005 on his ship the *Farley Mowat,* a 1958 Norwegian fishing research vessel named for the Canadian friend of sea mammals. The sea captain has had three vessels named after naturalists and animal advocates, including one called *The Cleveland Amory.* The latest is a 650-ton monster of ice-strengthened steel and offers a virtual tour of what Watson has done to build upon Amory's legacy over the past quarter century. Labyrinthian hallways and narrow stairways lead to the upper deck, where two Zodiaks are covered in tarps. These small, ninety-horsepower watercraft have been used by Watson's crew members, who have no qualms about putting themselves between whales and whalers with poised harpoons. Throughout the ship, stairway railings are decorated with knotted rope, longlines that Watson and his activists confiscated from the seas near Antarctica, New Zealand, Costa Rica, and around the globe. Each longline can stretch for seventy miles and floats at sea with baited hooks, entangling sharks, sea turtles, large fish, and birds. By pulling these lines before fishermen return, the crew has had much success releasing marine life back to freedom. In 2004, Watson commandeered an important mission to Taiji, a village in southern Japan where fishermen place sounding rods below the ocean surface to disorient dolphin and small whale sonar and to drive whole families and pods into shallow bays, where they are confined by a large net and speared until they bleed to death. This atrocity goes on every year from October to March in several small towns across Japan, killing thousands of dolphins and whales to feed a meat market that is not good at labeling the fish it sells to restaurants. Activists freed many Taiji dolphins from the bay, where the animals were held overnight to await the next morning's bloodbath, and consequently were jailed.

Watson hasn't changed much; he's still an irascible yet lovable figure who ventures where no one else dares to go. His hair has turned a little more white, like that of the baby harp seals. Watson has found today's seal hunt a bit different from the previous ones, as the sealers have become more violent—toward people. Several members of his international volunteer crew were attacked, punched, and struck with clubs, but none of the thugs were arrested by Canadian police, who were right there monitoring the hunt. When the crew took photographs of the sealers, they were arrested. Cruelty toward animals has been documented too: a group of international veterinarians who observed a hunt discovered that 79 percent of the sealers had failed to even try to determine if an animal was dead before skinning its body—sealers are first supposed to touch the eyes to see if they blink, indicating the seal is still conscious and alive. The vet team also performed postmortem examinations and learned that nearly half of the seal skulls had minimal or no fractures, suggesting that they were conscious during the skinning, a clear violation of Canada's marine mammal regulations. With a Department of Fisheries and Oceans that spends only 1.5 percent of its patrol hours monitoring sealers, it is no doubt that such violations go unpunished. But even when officials are present, there is no guarantee.

Some of the people involved in saving seals during Amory's time wonder if activists have what it takes to win this time. Watson observes that many good people are simply not willing to give up their comfortable lifestyle to a cause. International Fund for Animal Welfare founder Brian Davies, who has retired to Barnstable, Massachusetts, notes how much the world has changed since he became involved in the movement in the 1960s, and how much the pendulum has swung the other way. If Rebecca Aldworth is any example, the movement is in good shape and moving forward. One of Davies's former staff members in Montreal, Aldworth now works on the seal campaign in America. It is her job as the Humane Society's director of Canadian Wildlife Issues to graphically document the slaughter in her personal journals and distribute them to policymakers and the public. A native of Newfoundland, Aldworth remembers at five years old watching Amory on a TV show airing a documentary of the seal slaughter, and largely because of him she is committed to the movement for life. She believes that it will take heavy political and public pressure worldwide to stop the hunt, and that the United States must pressure Canada's prime minister, especially now that his country is reportedly prodding American politicians into reopening the seal market in the States. Aldworth has long promoted Davies's innovative idea to convince Canada of the benefits of turning its government-sponsored seal killing into government-backed seal-watching, a lucrative tourist attraction that could help its economy.

Seal killer just moments before striking with a hakapik, spring 2005 (Brian Skerry, the Humane Society of the United States)

While the seal hunt grows beyond our borders, overall hunting in the United States has seen a steady decline, a loss of more than 1 million hunters, or 1 percent, each year since the 1990s. The bulk of hunters are white males in their fifties and sixties, a shrinking population, and at this rate, demographers say, sport hunting will be extinct by 2050. Activists believe that time is on their side, even while the industry is making a push, in one organizer's words, to breed outside the kennel. First the industry appealed to women with the nationwide Becoming an Outdoors Woman program, telling wives and particularly single mothers how to strengthen the bonds of family by picking up a rifle. Because women are not doing so in great numbers, the industry has turned to children, with several attempts to lower the legal hunting age. As studies show, kids who don't hunt by age four-teen are not apt to hunt at all, and therefore states are cutting rates for junior license fees and holding special hunts for children, such as the Oregon Department of Fish and Wildlife's recent mother-child rabbit hunt and Connecticut's invitation to pick off pen-raised pheasants. Agencies are adamant about calling them youth hunts rather than chil-dren's hunts, just as they call killing harvesting, but semantics cannot hide what a child sees after pulling the trigger. With the legal age to hunt as low as eight years old, a child is too young to drink, too young to vote, and too immature to drive but can pick up a high-powered rifle and blast the life out of an animal. The Fund and the Humane Society are fighting this new push wherever it appears, by promoting legislation to raise the legal age. The issue was important to Amory, who wrote many articles about fostering a child's natural affinity with animals by teaching respect, rather than brainwashing them to believe that animals are nothing more than moving targets and that violence is an acceptable form of entertainment. By now, every state has an out-reach program for children to save hunting, a huge issue for today's activists.

While urban cultural trends suggest that hunting could lose its edge among youth, as they are more interested in video games, music, and outdoor sports with a ball, hunters are rallying to reinstate hunts banned long ago. New Jersey just held its first black bear hunt in thirty-one years to appease hunters eager for a skin rug or head on a wall, as well as residents, who have encroached onto bear habitat and are com-plaining of pesky bruins knocking over their garbage, damaging their cars, and getting into birdfeeders. It's a growing conflict in sprawling mountain developments and burgeoning suburbs, created by people who see it as a one-sided—bear—problem. And it is frustrating for wildlife managers who hear from people like the woman who moved into the mountains, saw a bear lumbering across her backyard, and called to say, "You don't just let them run wild, do you?" Biologists argue that shooting random bears is akin to solving crime by firing into a crowded room, and in fact can make things worse by removing the biggest and best, leaving room for immature males to expand their ter-ritory and turn into problem bears.[3] Maryland, as well, recently brought back the bear hunt after fifty-one years, though there has never been a bear attack in the state. In Michigan, after a century of protecting mourning doves—the state's designated bird of peace—hunting groups persuaded lawmakers to add them to the list of flying targets. And for the first time in three decades, Pennsylvania now allows hunters to trap or shoot bobcats—a shy, elusive animal not much bigger than a housecat—which haven't bothered anyone. No one hunts a feline predator for food, and the bobcat does not spread disease. In fact it helps farmers by eating mice that get into grain. Without a survey of populations, the state gave in to hunters who wanted, in one spokesman's words, "a new recreational opportunity."

Animal activists see their present challenge as one of image and awareness. People may learn to solve their own bear problems if they are educated about coexisting with wildlife and agree to take some responsibility by storing trash in bearproof containers, by not leaving pets and pet food outside, especially overnight, by keeping smelly diapers inside, by cleaning their barbecue grills, by forgoing bird feeders, and in general by not doing anything to lure wildlife to their homes. To save Michigan's mourning doves, the Fund and the Humane Society have gathered enough signatures—more than 275,000—and public support to put the issue on the 2006 ballot and let voters decide whether to ban dove shoots permanently. To halt the slaughter of tens of thousands of American horses each year, Pacelle and Markarian are pushing federal legislators to pass the American Horse Protection Act. Those who speak for animals have already logged in some major wins. When North Carolinians learned in 2004 about the brutality of cockfighting for money and the crime it brought to their communities, lawmakers passed a felony bill. When socially aware corporations and universities realized that the public frowns on keeping hens confined in small battery cages, they signed on to a pledge to stop buying and selling eggs from such places. And when Indianans became savvy to the secret world of canned hunts, their state wildlife agency banned all such operations, which numbered about 350.

Canned hunts, also called game farms or game ranches—or as operators like to call them, hunting preserves or shooting preserves—are private ranches where landowners invite unlicensed hunters to take their pick of big-game animals. It's a luxury getaway for the rich and idle, who are led by a guide who knows the whereabouts, day or night, of every animal inside a barricade of wire and steel, resembling prison grounds. After a good night's sleep in a luxury lodge, the hunter is handed a high-powered rifle, given a quick tutorial, and driven up to

Seal campaign leader Rebecca Aldworth on the ice with seal pup, 2005 (Brian Skerry, the Humane Society of the United States)

the animal to release the trigger or bow. It may be a lion sleeping under a shade tree, a wildebeest at a waterhole, or an oryx grazing. There are an estimated 4,000 such operations in twenty-five states, the most numerous being in Texas, followed by Michigan, Pennsylvania, Florida, Colorado, Ohio, Missouri, Maine, Tennessee, and Louisiana. In Texas alone, 230,000 exotic animals encompassing 124 species wander former cattle ranches and farms, where landowners charge anywhere from $1,500 to $12,500 for an individual kill. These animals come from zoos, are retired circus performers, or are bought from private breeders and wildlife dealers. Some are endangered species that came to the United States for a captive breeding program and wound up in a captive killing program instead.[4] Some operations have split their acreage in two, with half for shooting safaris and half for photo safaris, but hunters can choose any animal, even those on the photo safari side, as someone will move the animal across the partition. Needless to say, there is no fair chase in canned hunts and no physical effort—a standard among ethical hunters—for doing something about as grueling as getting a beer from the refrigerator.

Seal killers approaching (Kathy Milani, the Humane Society of the United States)

Canned hunts date back to the 1920s, when the King Ranch in southern Texas released nilgai, a type of antelope from Asia, on its compound. A decade later, the San Antonio Zoo became a partner with Texas ranchers, sharing ungulates that came in off the boats. But it was sport hunting that spurred canned hunts as a commercial venture, write Elizabeth Cary Mungall and William J. Sheffield in their book, *Exotics on the Range.* In the 1950s, ranchers and farmers were hit by a severe seven-year drought and soon invited hunters onto their lands and paid them to shoot wildlife for dollars. One of the first ranches to do this was the Y. O. in Mountain Home, near San Antonio, which released Indian blackbuck antelopes in 1953, then added axis, sika, and fallow deer. Soon exotic wildlife spread well beyond Texas' borders and was dubbed alternative livestock.

It is clear that people do not engage in canned hunts for the meat, as a weekend trip can cost $1,600. One operation, the Diamond K Ranch in Texas, reports giving away 5,000 pounds of unclaimed meat every year. Operators have had much success keeping their businesses under the radar—that is, until Markarian's staff captured on videotape the hideous death of a defenseless, declawed, and terrified black leopard. The big cat was bottle-fed and raised not to fear humans until the day he was stuffed into a cage and surrounded by hunters who came to a Texas cow pasture to kill him. The men poked their guns through the cage holes to agitate the animal, but once the door was sprung, the leopard did not rush to the fields as they had expected. He acted more like a frightened housecat and cowered in the corner. Someone kicked the cage and the leopard slinked under a pickup truck. Dogs were set loose to flush him out. Overwhelmed by the pack, the cat turned belly up, feebly pawing until the shooter walked up and fired. The videotape was played on national news.

More stories came to light. In California three Bengal tigers, three cougars, and two leopards were shot in their cages, some as they were walking out. NBC exposed the shooting of a sleeping tiger and a helpless lion. Activists documented the killing of a Corsican ram who ran up against a wire fence while being chased by a hunter, who then pumped her body with six arrows while she slowly, painfully died. A head shot would have ruined the trophy.

Canned hunts are no different from a slaughterhouse, with one exception: the killers have fun and somebody gets rich. The advertisements say it all. One operation in New York reads: "Tired of traveling, spending money and coming home with nothing to show for it? Book your successful trophy hunt today!" Another one in Texas: "We put 40 lbs of corn at each stand twice a week so the deer and hogs are used to coming to them. You may put out corn at the stand you are hunting to attract boar and javelina. We have 36 comfortable box stands." Another ranch boasts of having hunting stands that tower over mineral licks and timer-controlled feeders. And one called Covenant Ranch Macho Bucks claims that it has "passion for caring for God's creatures" and tells hunters, "The results will blow you away! The deer never knew what hit them!" What the ads don't say, however, is how the animals are manipulated in every way to ensure a kill. They are baited, even tied up, or drugged. There is no federal law regulating canned hunts, and they are legal in all but fourteen states: California, Delaware, Georgia, Massachusetts, Minnesota, Montana, Nevada, New Jersey, North Carolina, Oregon, Virginia, Washington, Wisconsin, and Wyoming. These operations stay afloat because of the greed of state governments for the billions of dollars they bring in and because of support from the Farm Bureau and the Institute for Agricultural and Trade Policy, which calls canned hunts the crop of the future. Safari Club International awards shooters coveted prizes for killing many animals of diverse species. Anyone can earn the "Dangerous Game of Africa" title for shooting a lion and any of a slew of other animals without leaving the country or ever breaking a sweat. Activists are working for a federal ban against such vile exploitation of exotic animals. They are also disturbed about something called Internet hunting, in which people aim a mounted gun with the click of the mouse and kill an animal without ever stepping outdoors.

Despite witnessing so many horrors perpetrated on animals, Amory never gave up the fight. The idea never crossed his mind. Animal work is a field that can be terribly discouraging and make one want to throw in the towel, but Amory taught by example, which sustained those around him. He attracted people who, like himself, could bounce back. All that he asked is that they, too, always believe that every cause is winnable, and so is the whole war. If Amory had one regret, it was that it took too long to make positive change and society was too slow to protect animals. His protégés believe that stronger communication will help the Animal Rights movement gain momentum. Markarian envisions a greater effort in advertising, something akin to pervasive public service announcements against smoking cigarettes, but his group will saturate the market with a message of compassion rather than personal health. Celebrities will continue to be an important element. Movie stars Adrien Brody, Kevin Bacon, and Pierce Brosnan, among others, recently answered the call to stage a fundraising event for the seal campaign by signing T-shirts to raise awareness. An actress in the film *Thumbsucker* wore a Humane Society T-shirt in one scene bearing the words "Club Sandwiches Not Seals." The director even placed a link to the seal campaign on the film's website.

Pacelle, Markarian, and their army of advocates plan to take Amory's legacy to a whole new level, using the same broad-based arsenal of resources to target politics, the law, and the media, while holding the same goal of creating a kinder society. It will require fantastic effort for this new generation to demand change. Perhaps, some in the movement muse, the world needs another Cleveland Amory to expose the evils, to make people accountable, and, as Watson says, to make a large enough portion of the 6 billion people on the planet "give a damn" about something besides themselves. Maybe someday

Wild mustangs saved from slaughter now at Cleveland Amory's Black Beauty Ranch. The government's roundup and accepted slaughter of America's horses remains a key campaign issue for today's activists. (D. J. Schubert, The Fund for Animals)

another person will come along, someone as flamboyant and colorful as Amory, a young dynamic individual willing to give his or her life to the cause. For now, dedicated animal advocates go about their workday doing their part to improve the world, inspired to keep one man's vision alive. Every day they walk past a huge poster, taped to the wall outside The Fund for Animals offices, bearing the confident face of their former leader cheek to cheek with Polar Bear, a photo that graced the cover of a 1990 *Parade* magazine. Amory is always present, and he continues to drive their work. They know he's still watching and pulling those strings.

Acknowledgments

Researching Cleveland Amory's work for animals set me on a wonderful journey where I met the most kind and dedicated people who are truly making the world a better place. First, I want to acknowledge Marian Probst, because without fail, every person I interviewed pointed out that it was Marian who ran The Fund for Animals all those times when Cleveland was away on speaking trips, field campaigns, and book tours. She was the first person he spoke to in the morning at work, and the last one before he headed home at night. Marian likes to say, "I'm just a secretary," but I immediately got a sense of what a strikingly sharp woman she is the first time I called the Fund's New York office to inquire about writing this book. Always one step ahead of me, Marian guided me toward the right person to contact next, and maintained the integrity of the story. I appreciate her sense of humor and zest for life, which made for fun and lively conversations. Much appreciation to Wayne Pacelle for putting me in touch with Marian and setting this three-year project into motion.

When I began, I was still working as an editorial writer for the *Daily Camera* in Boulder. Without the support of its former publisher Colleen Conant, and editor Cindy Sutter, I would not have had the necessary flexibility to pursue this labor of love. Also much thanks to fellow journalists and authors Clay Evans, Juliet Wittman, and Larry Tye for their invaluable guidance and sound advice along the way. I would not have continued if I didn't have a book contract in hand, so my heartfelt thanks goes to Stephen Topping, who was the first one to believe in me as a book writer. I am indebted to my publisher, Mira Perrizo, who continued to share that faith and clearly believed in the merits of this particular project. I thank her for allowing me and encouraging me to savor the freedom of having my own voice—something journalists are loath to do. I am grateful for the contributions of Robert Sheldon, formerly of Johnson Books, for his creativity, expertise, and enthusiasm. And to Linda

Doyle who "came late to the dinner table": you inspire me with your boundless energy, compassion, and understanding.

As someone who prefers to hear great stories from those individuals who were actually there, I felt compelled to travel, and am forever grateful to Paul Watson and Allison Lance-Watson of Sea Shepherd Conservation Society, for being so generous with their time while their ship was docked in Seattle for repairs. I am in awe of their enduring strength to combat what is one of the largest evils done by humans on this planet. I also felt very privileged to have interviewed the venerable Brian Davies, who founded the International Fund for Animal Welfare, and was an equal partner in the first wave of fighting the baby seal slaughter. A very special thanks to rodeo champion and career cowboy Dave Ericsson, for his amazing hospitality at his Arizona cattle ranch, and for teaching me to (gently) rope a cow, or to at least try. As he liked to say, "If it were easy, women would do it." (Very funny, Dave.) And thank you to D. J. and Janet Schubert, for handing me the keys to the open-topped, archaic orange jeep to tool around Black Beauty Ranch and experience the animals alone and on their terms. As soon as I could figure out the gear shift, it was a memorable way to see Cleveland's legacy alive and well in East Texas. Thanks to Alfredo Govea, Loree Roberts, Dawna Epperson, and everyone at the ranch who has the distinct privilege of spending their days in the most peaceful, heavenly place. And tremendous thanks to Michael Markarian and Heidi Prescott for their openness and kindness, for allowing me to observe a Fund for Animals anti-hunting meeting, and for sharing some of their precious staff's time to help me dig into their mountains of files in the former Silver Spring office.

My research went smoothly because of the incredible efficiency and professionalism of the staff at the Boston Public Library. Special thanks to Mary Beth Dunhouse, as well as Megan Fleming and Eric Frazier. And thanks to Colleen Hyde of the Grand Canyon Museum Collection, for her invaluable assistance in ferreting out the right transcripts, videotapes, and documents for the burro rescue. Although that chapter is critical of the 1980s Park Service, I hope she remains interested in seeing the whole story on the shelves in the museum and gift shop. I also want to thank Jim Walters, who was one of the first people I interviewed, for his splendid candor on the agency's plan to just shoot the burros. It is rare and refreshing to find a government worker who is so bravely honest when speaking for publication.

I am grateful to so many people who not only opened their hearts to share their Cleveland stories, but were willing to temporarily part with their precious, priceless photographs and memorabilia. Thank you to Cindy Traisi of the Wildlife Rehabilitation Center, for sending me incredible slides and photographs of raptors and coyotes she has released, as well as wonderful shots of Cleveland with the San Clemente goats and multiple felines. I am sure that it was tough for her to find time in the midst of so many mouths to feed. And thank you to Doris Dixon, for trusting me with her only tape bearing a telephone machine message from Cleveland—a rare personal treasure—and to Vicki Claman for her burro photos, and Dave Ericsson for his irreplaceable burro roundup albums and signed copy of *Man Kind?* Everything I have gathered is testimony to a man who was so well loved and respected. Also thanks to Grace Van Vleck, Beth McNulty, Julia Peirce Marston, and everyone at The Fund for Animals and the Humane Society, especially for their help with photographs, and thanks to photographer Raymond Eubanks.

This book is, for me, a tribute to my family. I am forever grateful to my willing and unwitting research assistants and parents, Bob and Barbara Hoffman, for spending long hours in the library watching videotape of Cleveland, reading and copying files. I do believe that kindness may be genetic, and so loving gratitude goes to my grandfather, Morey Rumaner, who long ago witnessed a man throwing a sack full of meowing kittens into a lake, and promptly dived into the water to save them. I think if Cleveland had known, he would have signed my grandfather to represent upstate New York. A world of love to my husband, Tim, for sharing my passion for animals, for caring about my goals, and for putting up with a missing wife, often into the wee hours. And to my cats, for not walking across the keyboard during crucial moments, and to my dogs for dealing with late dinners.

I am so honored that Wayne Pacelle joined me in this project. I first met Wayne when he came to Colorado to promote our state's successful measure to ban leg-hold traps. I continue to be in awe of his persuasive public speaking abilities, intellect, and generous spirit. Animal advocates are fortunate to have such a knowledgeable and clearheaded leader for the future. And finally, most of all, a universe of gratitude to Cleveland Amory, who opened my eyes and showed me that the possibilities are endless, that no one owns the script to how we treat animals, and that it can be rewritten. All it takes is courage and strength to stand up to those who think they have the power out of habit, and to say no, not this time, and never again.

Notes

Chapter 1

1. Curry College president Kenneth Quigley, his wife Beth, and their children live in the former Amory home. After seven years of living there, Beth Quigley was curious about its history and ran across a groundskeeper who had done some research. The home was remodeled in 1922, rebuilt in 1930, and later renovated, but had retained much of its original character and charm, including a library featuring built-in wooden bookshelves that stretch from ceiling to floor and a solarium with original, handmade Italian mosaic tile, as well as a ceramic fountain with carved stone cherubs. The house sits at the end of a winding, gravel road that ends in a circular drive. A few short steps from the doorway is an early 1900s horse stable, now used as a garage. Inside the front door is an inviting stairway with turned balusters. To the immediate right is the dining room, still with original, hand-painted wallpaper between the wainscoting and plastered ceiling, which came from a business called Zuber Bros. of Alsace Lorraine. The wallpaper is a virtual tour of the Boston Tea Party and historic American battles. To the left of the stairway is a large library built of warm, dark woods including mahogany bookshelves stacked, wall to wall, with what appear to be early collections of hardbound classics by famous writers such as Mark Twain. "We use this house a lot for college events," Beth Quigley says, standing on her flagstone terrace surrounded by a sloping hillside of lush, wild ivy. "It's part of campus, but it feels private and so it has been a perfect fit for honoring guests at fund-raising events."

2. Amory's investigation into animal experimentation exposed a secondary topic, stealing pets to supply laboratories, which immediately thrust the issue into the mainstream because it would now affect anyone with a beloved pet. The scenario demeans the very foundation of love, trust, faith, and loyalty upon which all relationships—among all species—are based, Amory argued before a congressional committee. "Are we all head and no heart? Are we all

science and no humanity? Are we so consumed with ourselves that we no longer have even pity for any of God's other creatures?" Lawmakers were willing to listen and took sides with Amory in one hearing in which a Dr. Maurice Visscher, president of the National Society for Medical Research, argued that he needed "enough animals" for research. Senator Warren Magnuson, a Democrat from Washington, replied, "You don't need my dog, do you? She'd bite you, she would."

3. Leinhardt is the daughter of Amory's second wife, actress Martha Hodge. (He married his first wife, Cora Fields Craddock, in 1941.) The couple separated after twenty-two years of marriage in 1975 and were divorced in 1977. Amory's surviving family includes Leinhardt, a University of Pittsburgh professor of education, and her twenty-seven-year-old daughter, Zoe. Amory's brother Robert had two sons, Daniel and Robert, and three grandsons, and all the cousins remain very close. One of the lessons Leinhardt has passed on to her daughter she learned from Amory: it's worth the risk to put intense energy into whatever you are doing and know that it's okay to fail. After all, Amory wrote theater scripts that never panned out, but he "still worked with the same gusto that he put into everything else."

Chapter 2

1. Amory was a master at capturing a crowd. Animal rights organizer Henry Spira talked about the time he heard Amory spin a magical tale. "I saw him on a train on the way to Washington once. In no time, he had everyone in the car wrapped around his finger, telling stories about himself. By the end, he was passing out his leaflets, and he even got a donation from one guy."

2. Dixon wrote a book, *Memoirs of a Compassionate Terrorist* (1998), to reach people who may not yet be animal activists but can relate to her many adventures with The Fund for Animals.

3. Regenstein is author of many books on wildlife and the environment, including *The Politics of Extinction, The Shocking Story of the World's Endangered Wildlife* (1975); *America the Poisoned: How Deadly Chemicals Are Destroying Our Environment, Our Wildlife, Ourselves—and How We Can Survive!* (1982); and *Replenish the Earth: A History of Organized Religion's Treatment of Animals and Nature* (1991).

4. Henry Bergh also was founder of the first Society for the Prevention of Cruelty to Children. It has always been common for detractors of the humane movement to claim that animal welfarists are interested only in animals and

that this work detracts from the welfare of children: if you care for animals, somehow you are a child-hater. Amory wrote a compelling case against such poor logic in a *Christian Science Monitor* essay, "From Human Society to Humane Society," in which he pointed out that the first parent ever prosecuted for cruelty to a child was prosecuted under the law that Bergh had fought for to protect animals. Amory vehemently argued that those in the organized humane movement are not just for animals for *animals*. "We are for animals for *people*," because less cruelty to animals means less cruelty to people. One could say Amory was ahead of the curve, since today it is widely accepted by law enforcement that harmful acts against animals can be a predictor of violence, particularly domestic violence against women.

5. A detailed history of the Animal Rights movement can be found in Bernard Unti's book, *Protecting All Animals: A Fifty-Year-History of the Humane Society of the United States* (2004). Unti, a historian, wrote his doctoral dissertation on the animal cruelty movements of the late nineteenth and early twentieth centuries.

6. A Boston Public Library worker who was sorting through Amory's belongings to create a catalog for his collection says she found the dog tags of Tyrone Power, a famous actor and heartthrob of the 1930s to 1950s. Amory and his star connection seems to turn up everywhere. Virginia Handley has taken to writing down any reference to Amory she stumbles across, the latest being Caroline Kennedy Schlossberg's biography, in which Amory is mentioned three times. She discovered that Amory had dated Katharine Hepburn's sister and knew Tallulah Bankhead, Dorothy Parker, and Jackie Kennedy. Some stars were devoted animal advocates, such as Doris Day, who founded her own animal rights organization, called the Doris Day Animal League.

Chapter 3

1. In 1971, Watson, an environmentalist, cofounded the Don't Make a Wave Committee, charged with the sole mission of opposing the atomic bomb. One year later, Watson renamed his organization the Greenpeace Foundation and rededicated its efforts to include the end of whaling. Much of Watson's tribulation with Greenpeace can be read in his book, *Seal Wars: Twenty-five Years on the Front Lines with the Harp Seals* (2003).

2. While Amory, Watson, and the crew stayed in Boston to ready their ship, there was need for many trips to the grocery and hardware stores, and the sea captain was encouraged to make use of Amory's quirky converted Checker

cab. "It was funny," Watson says. "I'd stop the car at a light and someone would get in the back seat."

3. The Norwegian name for the harp seal is *Selhund*, which means "sea dog." The French say *loup-marin*, which means "sea wolf." The origin of the harp seal is debatable, but some scientists believe that the animal evolved from a doglike ancestor from the North Pacific.

4. More details can be read in Watson's book, *Ocean Warrior: My Battle to End Illegal Slaughter on the High Seas* (1994). As of this writing, a film with the same working title is being shot on location in Canadian waters and a studio tank in Mexico (where *Titanic* was filmed), and Amory is one of the characters, because he was extremely important to Watson and essential to changing people's minds about sea animals, says L.A. film producer Pieter Kroonenburg. "I very much wanted to make an action-adventure film that would highlight Paul's exploits. ... This is a wonderful story, you have a man named Cleveland, who sticks his neck out to make a difference."

Chapter 4

1. Ericsson has kept the same bloodline since before the mid-1970s. Stinger, the main dog working his ranch today, is Jake's great-grandson. A tan dog with long legs, a broad head, and a skinny long tail that wags to greet visitors to the ranch, Stinger looks something like a lanky pit bull, but "there's no bull in him, he's all hound," Ericsson says. "And he knows more about cows than most people."

2. It was not a Walt Disney movie ending, says Walters, who moved on to Santa Fe, New Mexico, where he became the Park Service's deputy Wilderness Program coordinator. He claims that after the Fund's burro rescue, park rangers discovered a few remaining "dumb ones," frightened by helicopters and cowboys, and hiding deep in the canyon. These animals, numbering about thirty, were later shot by the rangers. Additionally, during the rescue some pregnant females were spooked by the chase and aborted.

3. Although the animals are long gone, Park Service biologists have reminders of the burros, whose wide hooves trampled archaeological sites and fouled waterholes. "The land has still not healed," Ward says. "The effects are still visible."

4. Amory's disdain for the Park Service lingered once he heard that park visitors were being told that the burros were rescued not by his Fund for Animals, but by the federal rangers.

Chapter 5

1. Amory was a relentless advocate for burros; in the week before he died, he found more burros in the West and began calling around to his field agents for help to find them homes.

2. More than 50,000 mares on 500 farms, mainly in North Dakota and Minnesota, exist to produce Premarin, an estrogen product extracted from pregnant mares' urine and used in hormone replacement therapy. According to the Humane Society of the United States, the Premarin industry not only is cruel in warehousing pregnant mares but also creates 35,000 "surplus" foals every year, many of which are sent to slaughter.

3. Government bureaucrats that claim wild horses damage vegetation, pollute water, and threaten other species. Such claims, if true, allow the agency to get rid of "excess" animals if they are, in fact, causing ecological damage. But in 1982 a National Academy of Science study concluded there was no basis for these claims: "We have seen very few areas with heavy vegetation impact, although we have asked the BLM to show them to us." The General Accounting Office in 1990 reported that there is no evidence to indicate that moving off large numbers of horses has indeed affected the land. Horses and burros, in fact, benefit the environment, says the Fund's former Rocky Mountain coordinator, Andrea Lococo, whom Amory hired in 1990 to take on this issue. Their digestive system allows whole seeds to be eliminated and dispersed into the environment. Their hooves plant the seeds and blaze trails during heavy snowfalls, and they break ice during winter freezes, helping predators and scavengers find food. Still, the bureau maintains there are too many horses and made its pitch to Congress. In 2000, lawmakers allocated $9.6 million to increase roundups by 50 percent.

4. In 1986 the Fund first won an injunction in a Nevada federal district court against the bureau, forcing it to withhold title from those who intended to slaughter adopted horses. Two years later the ruling was upheld by the Ninth Circuit Court of Appeals in San Francisco. The injunction was later modified to include the affidavit.

5. These horses were caught in the midst of a nasty dispute between the bureau, which claimed the animals were trespassing by grazing on public lands, and members of the Western Shoshone Tribe, who say these lands belong to the tribe and the horses should remain. The Fund's threat of a lawsuit won some time to delay the roundup, and eventually the Fund was able to find other sanctuaries to take the entire herd.

6. Chimpanzees are thought to be humankind's closest cousins, and yet thousands are bred to serve in laboratory experiments. They live in concrete cages and are taken out only to be poked and prodded or to undergo surgery for infectious disease, spinal and brain injury research, or toxicity testing. The journal *Nature* counters the notion that culture—behaviors learned through observation as opposed to inheritance—is uniquely human. An international team of primatologists, including Jane Goodall, pooled 151 years of observational research and found thirty-nine behaviors that could only have been adopted through learning and imitation. Researchers found that chimp greetings, courting styles, and even rain dances varied among chimps, much as learned behaviors vary in human communities.

Chapter 6

1. US Representative Bobbi Fiedler, a Republican from Northridge, was an ally of The Fund for Animals, arguing alongside Amory in meetings with Secretary of Defense Caspar Weinberger. No doubt it also helped that Amory's longtime friend, Benjamin Welles, was Weinberger's assistant.

2. The Fund for Animals' Operation Goat rescue had the help of Fund executive director Jerry Owens and John Price, Jr., as crew members.

3. Patricia Nelson founded the Animal Trust Sanctuary and, when she was eighty years old, she took in seventy-seven goats rescued from San Clemente Island, before donating her shelter to The Fund for Animals.

4. Cindy Traisi shares detailed accounts of some of the fascinating animals she has met in her book, *Because They Matter...* (1997).

Chapter 7

1. The Hegins pigeon shoot also became the subject of a Newbery Medal–winning children's book, *Wringer* (1997) by Jerry Spinelli, who writes about a nine-year-old boy who musters the courage not to become a wringer—Trapper Boy—and hides a pet pigeon in his bedroom.

2. Death in bow hunting results from loss of blood or an infection following loss of blood. In his 1989 book, *The Bowhunting Alternative*, Texas bow hunter Adrian Benke exposes the problems of the method, for example the randomness of the arrow's landing. If it strikes far from the heart and lungs, he writes, it can take twelve hours of bleeding until death comes. The Texas Parks and Wildlife Department reported that beyond the 128 deer killed by

bow hunters in that state in the past thirteen years, an additional 130 others were wounded and never retrieved by the hunter. As a rule of thumb, for every deer shot and killed by a bow hunter, another deer is shot and wounded and dies in pain.

3. The Congressional Sportsmen's Caucus is made up of some of the nation's political leaders who are pro-hunting activists. They support canned hunts and trophy hunts, and their offices look like a shooting gallery. The office of Congressman John Dingell of Michigan sported a wild boar he shot himself, deer heads, two elk racks, two antelope horns, a duck, trout, and sailfish. A buffalo head adorned the office of Bill Paxon of upstate New York. New Hampshire senator Judd Gregg did his job beneath the head of a bull moose, while Oklahoma's Bill Brewster had wild turkeys. The winner is Don Young of Alaska with his Alaskan Kodiak bearskin and gray wolf pelt. Amory explained, "They've got to exhibit their macho, because if they don't, they'll be found out for what they are—outright cowards." Young, cochair of the Sportsmen's Caucus and chair of the House Committee on Natural Resources, replied with the charming demeanor befitting such a leader: "I could knock him on his ass any day of the week."

4. A 1995 Associated Press poll, conducted by ICR Survey Research Group of Media, Pennsylvania, asked residents in ten cities for their opinions about the use of animals in a variety of ways. The result was widespread support for animal rights beliefs. Two-thirds of 1,004 Americans polled agreed that "an animal's right to live free of suffering should be just as important as a person's right to live free of suffering." Two-thirds said it is seldom or never right to use animals in testing cosmetics, 59 percent said killing animals for fur is always wrong, and 51 percent said sport hunting is always wrong.

5. The Fund for Animals created a thirty-minute video called *What's Wrong with Hunting* that is a lesson available to teachers. In the video, Alexandra Paul of the TV show *Baywatch*, Tiffani-Amber Thiessen of *Beverly Hills 90210,* and Craig Paquette of the Kansas City Royals counter the notion of sport hunting for fun. The video is a response to wildlife agencies that have been a strong presence in schools; thirty-seven states sanction hunter training as part of the junior high or high school curriculum. Shooting sports groups had a foot in the door, spreading their messages with the aid of federal grants. When The Fund for Animals applied for such grants to tell another side, its applications were rejected.

6. The last passenger pigeon died in 1914 at the Cincinnati Zoo.

7. After earning a soiled reputation, this agency changed its name to Wildlife Services as a public relations move. Its core mission has remained the same, however, as it was responsible for exterminating a record 2.7 million animals in 2004—an increase of 1 million over 2003—which equals five dead animals per minute at taxpayer expense.

8. This photograph was published in *U.S. News & World Report*, February 5, 1990.

9. Mary Meagher, a brucellosis expert and National Biological Survey scientist who studied the buffalo for more than three decades, calls the fears of the cattle industry "completely unfounded."

10. A laboratory test reported by one of the slaughterhouses, C&C Meats, showed that only 2 of 200, or 1 percent of bison tested positive for brucellosis.

Chapter 8

1. In 1998 during an eighteen-month undercover investigation, the Humane Society, working with independent journalists, uncovered dogs and cats being ruthlessly slain in Asia to make fur clothing sold abroad, including America. DNA tests concluded that at least 480 coats lined with dog fur were being sold at Burlington Coat Factory, a chain of 225 stores in forty-two states. Dog fur toys were discovered at a gift shop at Ronald Reagan Washington National Airport. More than 2 million dogs and cats—both bred and strays—are killed annually in Asia for their fur. One video from China depicts about a dozen dogs living in a dirty shack, where skinned dogs hang from the ceiling; one dog is put in a sack and dragged outside; after hanging the dog by a stiff wire attached to a fence, a man grabs the dog's right rear leg, takes out a knife, and slashes it; the animal howls and struggles to free itself, as the man begins to skin the live animal. A video from the Philippines shows more than a dozen adult cats inside a bamboo cage; a man reaches into the cage and slips nooses around their necks and strings them up as they wriggle and cry; the man says he kills about seventy cats in a day. Thanks to this investigation, in 2000 Congress passed the Dog and Cat Protection Act, which of course is not enforceable outside the United States.

2. None of these hunters are indigenous people hunting for subsistence. Inuit or native people of the North hunt for ringed seals in the Arctic. In the Front region the last member of the Beothuk nation—an aboriginal society that relied on hunting and fishing—died in 1912; Newfoundlanders drove out the

Beothuk through a bounty hunt. They also drove out the Newfoundland wolf, walrus, and pilot whale from their territory, rendered the Labrador duck extinct, and extirpated the polar bear from their region.

3. The same situation applies to deer, considered by some to be another nuisance animal, but when deer populations are lowered, experts say, a phenomenon called twinning kicks in whereby does compensate by having not one but two offspring.

4. Activists argue that the importing of exotics also brings the risk of disease, including the fatal and incurable chronic wasting disease, a neurological disorder that kills elk and deer and has expanded into Colorado, Wyoming, and Nebraska and more recently into Illinois, New Mexico, South Dakota, and Wisconsin.

Index

Julie Hoffman Marshall is an award-winning journalist and longtime advocate for wildlife, pets, and the environment in her native state of Colorado. She has worked as an associate editor of the editorial pages, a features writer, and as an animal columnist for *The Daily Camera* in Boulder, Colorado. She reported on community news for *The Orange County Register* in Southern California, and was a public information officer for the Colorado Division of Wildlife. Ms. Marshall holds a master's degree in journalism from the University of Colorado at Boulder. She lives in Lafayette, Colorado, with her husband Tim and daughter Sarah. The Marshall home is run by two Malamutes—Moqui and Nakuma—and four cats—Simba, Kato, Inspector Clouseau, and Yogi.

Help us speak
for those who can't.

The Fund for Animals, founded in 1967, advocates for animals and provides care, veterinary treatment, spay and neuter services, and rehabilitation for rescued wildlife and companion animals at sanctuaries and rehabilitation centers from coast to coast, including our world-famous Cleveland Amory Black Beauty Ranch.

200 West 57th Street
New York, NY 10019
1-888-405-FUND
www.fundforanimals.org

The Fund for Animals
we speak for those who can't